The Love

Of

Daphnis & Chloe

~ and ~

5 Dafydd ap Gwilym poems

(c1320 to c1370)

Nigel Humphreys

editor Catherine Edmunds

Circaidy Gregory Press

Copyright information

paperback ISBN 978-1-906451-88-2
first published September 2015
ebook available in .mobi, ePub & .pdf formats

Printed in the UK
by Catford Print

Published by Circaidy Gregory Press
Creative Media Centre,
45 Robertson St, Hastings,
Sussex TN34 1HL

www.circaidygregory.co.uk

About the Author

Nigel Humphreys lives with Chris his wife and pet Labrador Lucy near Aberystwyth. He has had three collections of poetry published by Arbor Vitae Press (London) – 'The Hawk's Mewl' in in 2007, 'The Flavour of Parallel' 2010 and 'Of Moment' in 2013. For the last twelve years he has been irretrievably involved with the Poetry scene at The University Arts Centre and is a member of the Welsh Academy and Literature Wales.

nigelhumphreyspoet.webs.com

About Circaidy Gregory Press

Circaidy Gregory Press often produces titles by the winners and shortlisted authors from Earlyworks Press competitions, including fiction and poetry by the multi-talented editor of this book, Catherine Edmunds, the first of which was 'Small Poisons'…

"With charm, wit and magical style, Catherine Edmunds conjures a fairy tale for grown-ups, a fantasy with its feet firmly on the ground ... in a place where dreams and stark reality meet." – *Neil Marr, BeWrite Books*

Nigel Humphreys was the winner of the first ever Earlyworks Press poetry competition and his poem *Madonna Della Febbre* took pride of place in the anthology 'Routemasters & Mushrooms', which also contains works by Roger Elkin, Phil Fox and Sally Richards.

"a compilation that ranges from
the reassuringly familiar to the cosmic in scope.
Not a single bland, run-of-the-mill poem in the mix."
– *DJ Tyrer, Atlantean Publishing*

Circaidy Gregory has a varied poetry list including works by Sarah James, Marilyn Francis and Caron Freeborn and, for those who have enjoyed Humphreys' evocation of Ancient Greece, there is also R J Dent's intriguing version of 'Alcaeus' Poems & Fragments'…

"Alcaeus's nobility, conciseness and sweetness combine forcefully with his use of metaphor and his clarity."
– Dionysius of Halicarnassus, 'On Imitation'

"His poetry smells of vine-leaves and the sea." – Peter Levi, 'A History of Greek Literature'

www.circaidygregory.co.uk

Dedication

to

Peter Kay

for his initial invaluable help
and unstinting support
of this work

thanks also to

Non Evans

for her help with the Welsh translations

Editor's Introduction

Is *The Love Song of Daphnis & Chloe* a rollicking piece of fun or something quite sublime? In 1714 the Regent of France illustrated it with sketches of a highly suggestive nature, yet George Thornley in his translation of 1657 called it 'A Most Sweet and Pleasant Pastoral Romance for Young Ladies'. In 1857 Elizabeth Barrett Browning had her eponymous heroine *Aurora Leigh* call it an 'obscene text' with the result that it remained obscure for much of the nineteenth century, yet in 1831 Goethe was recommending it should be re-read once a year and calling it a masterpiece 'in which Understanding, Art and Taste appear at their highest point.'

I think it is all of that and more. George Thornley's translation is so sweet and delicate it manages to slip in the rude bits without anyone especially noticing, which must have delighted the young ladies who were being advised to read it. He treads a fine line, and as a result his version is witty and often tongue-in-cheek with a wonderful lightness of touch – but it's not quite the easy read it would have been in Thornley's day as there have inevitably been many linguistic changes since 1657. Luckily we now have this modern version by poet Nigel Humphreys, based on Thornley's translation and retaining its charm, but adding the poetry that has been missing in all previous versions – including, perhaps, the original. Longus, who penned the story in the first place, was a 'modern' who wanted to write something closer to a novel in order to keep up with the literary tastes of the day. Humphreys, however, is an Anglo-Welsh poet with music in his blood, and not only that – he lives in Penrhyn-coch, Ceredigion, birthplace of Welsh medieval poet Dafydd ap Gwilym. He was hardly going to give us a straight prose version. Instead, we have something utterly unique: a version of *Daphnis and Chloe* that could well be the longest *cywydd* ever written in either English or Welsh.

Humphreys knew little of the story when on a whim he picked up a reprint of Thornley's translation in a second-hand bookshop in Hereford for £1.50. This pastoral love story quickly blew him away with its sublime beauty. He started hunting out other versions, heading over to YouTube to watch Ravel's lyrical ballet version, *Daphnis & Chloé.* To his surprise, further research failed to come up with a poetry translation, so Humphreys set about writing his own, inspired by the poetry of Dafydd ap Gwilym. This medieval Welsh poet was an entirely appropriate model, not only because of his 'courtly love' style – he was strongly influenced by the troubadours of Provençe – but also because of his bawdy treatment of everyday life. Yes, it's Dafydd ap Gwilym who famously wrote a poem to his penis; a poem which was omitted from anthologies of his work until very recently because it was a rare editor who would have dared to include it. Humphreys has, needless to say, translated it, and that translation along with some other gems from ap Gwilym appears as a delightful extra at the end of this volume.

The form – *cywydd* – which Dafydd ap Gwilym made his own, comprises a series of seven syllable rhyming couplets written in *cynghanedd* (literally, 'harmony'), a term which refers to the sound-arrangement of stresses, alliteration and rhyme within each line. Humphreys has written in what purists might consider the wrong language for this form, using English rather than Welsh, but just as the Japanese *haiku*, has now been adapted to work in English, so has Humphreys adapted the Welsh *cywydd* by using his poetic skill to reproduce the essence of the original form without feeling the need to adhere to it slavishly. The Welsh harmony has been retained, partnered with an exquisite sense of what will work in English. This produces such delightful couplets as:

> four hives of fizzing bees,
> fifty sap-heavy apple trees,

I think what will astonish the modern reader most about *The Love Song of Daphnis & Chloe* is that here is a text, written originally in 'dog Greek' by Longus in the late second or early third century CE that continues to cast its spell over readers centuries later. It's a text that you can come to as an academic, interested to see how Theocritus' invention, *the Pastoral*, developed in later centuries, or how Longus used Aristotle's theories of 'unity'; or you can approach it as a Welsh medievalist, wondering how Dafydd ap Gwilym's legacy might translate into modern English; you can be a student of human sexuality and relationships; you can be a lover of the Rococo, or the paintings of Watteau – or you can simply be someone who enjoys an engagingly honest love story.

– C Edmunds December 2014

Contents

The ***Love Song*** *of* ***Daphnis & Chloe***

First Canto

Mitylene – city of Lesbos
for centuries honoured as
the island's fair chatelaine;
a distinguished domain
intersected by the sea
abounding with bridges weaned
of white polished marble.
You would not think to call
it a city but a moated land
within yet another island.

Some twenty furlongs away
the estate of a rich lord lay,
the most ideal idyllic terrain
under the eyes of Elysium.
There were ranges prodigal
with animals for game, hills
and vine-veined slopes, gilded
yields from corn-filled fields,
combes with orchards and lawns,
and pearl-strung hills, rich downs
with sheep, cattle and goats,
the sea trimming the coast
and to the horizon's far reach
the flourish of a burnished beach.

Lamo, a goatherd dwelling in
this serene land of Mitylene,
found one day an infant boy
lying naked in the meadows

in a secret grove serried by
fronds woven in vagrant ivy;
at its centre the grass bore
the babe as if the softest fur.
It was here that a goat came
almost every day to care
for the abandoned child
at some cost to its own kid.

Lamo noted the goat's comings
and goings and so, fearing
that its young starved alone,
he followed the goat at noon
and watched it carefully walking
around the frail foundling
lifting and planting its limbs
lest it tread recklessly
and maim it with its hooves.
He watched as the infant strove
to sup milk and suckle
as if from a mother's nipple;
and reeling at the scene
(as well he might) he drew near
and saw a beautiful boy child
in bonny health and beside
him precious highborn goods
subtly hinting at blue blood:
a small cloak dyed amethyst
fastened with a golden clasp
and by his side a knife, tiny
with a handle of polished ivory.

At first he thought of taking
away the valuable belongings
and abandoning the child. But
later, ashamed that he had not
matched the goat's charity,

he waited until night so that he
might bring them all to Myrtle,
his wife – the boy and chattels.

Lamo explained everything:
how he came across the foundling
exposed and suckling from a goat
and how ashamed and full of guilt
he could not bear the child
to die in that worthless wood.
So inveigling loyal Myrtle
he stowed away the chattels
and they took him to be theirs
with the goat as his wet nurse;
they agreed to call him Daphnis
so that he had a herder's alias.

Two years on another shepherd
from neighbouring fields
had the same luck, catching
his breath upon discovering
a parallel phenomenon.
A sacred Nymphaeum
lay in a domed cave known
as the Goddesses' sacred home;
their statues were sculpted
alluringly in stone, bare-footed
and bare-legged, their arms naked
to the shoulders, with wicked
hair shedding love everywhere;
their eyes and lips were smeared
with a honeyed cosmetic
drawn from love's very armoury;
and their thistle-down petticoats
were tied and tucked at the waist.
Together they were dressed
as if at a masque, yet statuesque.

The cave reached deep into rock
from where a chasm uncorked
a crystal fountain which soothed
eager streams greening the dew
of flowers before that holy place.
There, hung in high display
were the milk pails of fair maids,
and the pipes, whistles and reeds
of long-dead shepherds enshrined.
Times were when ewes wandered
into this cave and shepherds like
Dryas thought them lost for good;
so, training them to his purpose
he made a wicket to induce
and ensnare them in the cave.
But one day when he came
to candle his trap he chanced upon
a rare scene undreamed on:
as any mother might, a ewe
tenderly suckled a baby who
applied cherry lips tightly
first to one, then to the other teat;
and when the infant was full
the ewe nurse fussed it still,
licking and nudging it. The baby
was a girl and like Daphnis
found in finery with rich
hints of a genteel heritage.

On her head she wore a turban,
gold-embroidered and her pattens
were gilded as was her fine dress
and cloak. And because Dryas
thought this could not take place
without a god's good grace,
and learning charity from the ewe,
he cradled the infant, screwed

her chattels into his sack
and prayed to the Nymphs that
he might keep and happily rear
the poor scatterling in his care.
And so, when it was time to drive
his flocks home he told his wife
in their hovel all he had seen,
showed her the foundling, keen
for her to think of the baby
as her daughter and thereby
to nurse and nurture her
however unsure their future.

Nape was the mother's name
and, envious of the ewe, came
quickly to love the baby.
They called the infant Chloe,
a suitable peasant name,
and the infants grew apace
though their burgeoning beauty
was for everyone a mystery
their parents being hayseeds.

One night both Lamo and Dryas
dreamt of the Nymphs' cave
where its fountain cascades
into runnels and where Dryas
found Chloe. The Nymphs
took the infants with joy
to a comely but tyrannous boy –
he wore wings, bore a bow
and a quiver of small arrows.
The impish god pierced both
minikin hearts with the same bolt
decreeing that one must keep
goats and the other sheep.
At this their proxy fathers awoke

saddened by the Fates' joke
that Daphnis and Chloe would be
as them – herders with fleas –
despite their rich swaddlings.
It prompted them to bring
the best bread and cuts of meat
to their tables and to teach
their children the island tongue,
to disunite right and wrong
with other maidens and swains.

And so it was preordained –
decreed by divine intercession –
that they raise them as their own.
And having shared their dreams
and sacrificed by the stream
to the winged boy (whose name
remained unknown to them)
they introduced their children
to their work as herdsmen
with instructions over the way
to feed them before midday
and after sundown; and further
how to drive them to water
and back to the paddock,
which beast knew the crook
and which obeyed the voice.

Soon this fine young brace
of hill-herders were on fire
as if owning a great empire
and began to earn their keep
by treating their goats and sheep
kinder than others drovers did.
For Chloe owed her childhood
to a ewe and Daphnis to a goat.

Spring came and fields boasted
of rich colours, hills and valleys
filled with flowers, every lea
was green, fresh and perfumed.

Bees bumbling in the blossom,
stock doves wooing in the groves
and lambs leaping on the slopes
cheered every ear and eye.
And when such sights vied
in those blessed Elysian fields
the old and young copied
the surging world they heard
and saw, so that heeding birds
they whistled and chirped as well;
and seeing the lambs gambol
they danced on tripping toes;
to imitate the bees they chose
the boldest blooms and lobbed
them at each other ad-lib
or picked their petals to embellish
the statues of the sacred Nymphs.

Daphnis and Chloe were
forever bound together –
he herding and overseeing
straggling sheep while Chloe
drove her errant, bolder goats
back to the slopes from the coast.
Sometimes their flocks' freedom
from wolves was left to just one
of them alone while the other
played pebbles in the clover.
Their fun echoed the merriment
of puppies and peasant infants:
a giddy Chloe might gather up
windlestraws to plait and trap

a cricket, and being so intent
was therefore very often
heedless of her herd. Daphnis,
easily distracted too, was
forever cutting slender reeds,
fret-holing their stems and
banding them with resin
to make a pan flute; then
he would practise or compose
from early dawn to day-close.
They shared wine, milk, whatever
they had brought to the pasture
and you would more likely see
their animals in a mad stampede
than Chloe stray from Daphnis.

Yet, while in this state of bliss –
this delicious delectation –
love manoeuvred against their fun:
for a wolf often ventured there
in the fields, hungry from its lair
stealing their livestock to feed
its own howling litter's need.
And the villagers would meet
at well-chosen and discreet
sites to dig deep pits and fix
across them long, rotting sticks
over which they threw soil
so that a hare or wildfowl
running there would break
the laths which gave away
like stubble. To beast brains
these traps feigned firm terrain
and many such trench-snares
were dug in the hillside pasture.
Yet they could not take the wolf.
She was cunning enough

to recognise a trapdoor
and many sheep were gnawed
to death, and nearly Daphnis too
when the following ensued:

two billy goats began to fight –
their jousting was violent.
In the first furious clash
one goat's horn was smashed
and in panic he turned tail
his foe tight on his trail.
No time for breath Daphnis
coached by recklessness
took up his club and tracked
the victor down. But the act
of rushing away on impulse
often makes for dire results,
and the goat and then Daphnis
crashed into a trap, his fall
broken only by the animal.
Thus Daphnis came to grief
deep in the fake ditch as if
galloping on a wild goat.
And there – a sorry sight –
he quickly began to shout
for someone to pull him out.

Chloe, expecting the worst,
ran to cry over his corpse
but finding him still alive,
though buried as in a grave,
shouted too for a helping hand
from any passing herdsman.
One quickly came but no-
where could he find a rope
to heave him out, so Chloe,
much alarmed, in haste freed

her long hair and let it down.
Standing on firm ground
at the pit rim the two began
to heave and haul so that
Daphnis with a firm grip
on Chloe's make-do rope
rose like a dart to the top.
The goat in stricken shape
with horns badly broken
was rescued too and given
to the herdsman as a prize
for saving both their lives.

After returning to their flocks
found quietly grazing locked
into the ways of Lamo
they sat on an oak tree bole
and began to inspect
Daphnis for any marked effects
of his fall. But they found
nothing bruised and no blood;
only that his head, chest and
limbs were heavily marbled
by dark treacherous mud.
So they decided he should
wash in the Nymphs' Cave
before this bizarre close shave
was made known to his folk.
Once there he gave Chloe
his shredded clothes to hold
while he scrubbed head to toe,
and as he washed the thought
of her kisses cued this sport:

Why in the name of the Nymphs
am I driven mad by Chloe's kiss?
Her lips are softer than wild roses

in lush maytime meadows
or on honeydew lawns yet her kiss
stings like a bee. I have kissed
kid goats, Melampo's puppy
and the calf Dorco gave me
but this new kind of kiss
tempts me beyond innocence.
My heart leaps to my lips,
my spirit sparks, my soul flips
with madness to kiss her again.
Oh, what a devilish game
this is! What an infirmity
whose name is unknown to me!
Did Chloe take poison before
we kissed? So why, therefore,
is she not dead? How proudly
nightingales sing in the boughs
yet my pipe sulks mute in a tree!
How the young goats skip free
while I sit here ! How fertile
are the fields' flowers while
I stall to weave her garlands!
Violets, hyacinths and
gilded cowslips all flourish
while Daphnis languishes!
And could it be that Dorco in time
will seem fairer to Chloe than I?

Thus Daphnis felt such pangs
and for the first time the sting
and cruel agency of love.
Indeed when Dorco observed
Dryas planting young graftings
in his valley vineyard, he
slyly greeted him with cheeses
and sued for Chloe on his knees.
They were old friends from

their cattle-droving days together
so it was easy for Dorco to plead
for the hand of his daughter Chloe.

If he could have her as his wife
he would give Dryas many gifts
befitting a worthy husbandman:
for his plough a yoke of oxen,
four hives of fizzing bees,
fifty sap-heavy apple trees,
sound shoe-making leather
and a weaned calf every year.
Pleased with these gifts Dryas
wanted no more than to promise
Chloe. Yet reflecting further
he thought she deserved better,
and moreover he took fright
lest it ever came to light
that he had seized an infant
ritually exposed to the elements
and would then find himself
in great unnecessary grief.

And so he asked to be excused,
rejected the marriage and refused
the gifts. But Dorco, displeased
that his cheeses were sneezed
at, vowed to possess fair Chloe
if ever he caught her away
from her own people. Primed
that each day it was sometimes
Daphnis and sometimes Chloe
who drove out their flocks to feed
he devised a devious plan
worthy of the wiliest herdsman.
Skinning the hide of a wolf
killed by an angry bull's hoof

he flung it onto his back so it
stretched down to his feet,
the huge paws covered his hands,
its immense hind legs hanged
down his thighs to his heels
and its gaping mouth concealed
his head like a helmet.
Disguised as a wolf as best
he could, he made off
to the spring where the flocks
usually drank after grazing.
It glistered in a maze
of overgrown bracken, shrubs,
briars and bristling bushes
so that a wolf might indeed
creep there quite concealed.
And while waiting hidden
for Chloe's herd to be driven
there for watering he prized
the vain hope that disguised
as this fierce wanton wolf,
he'd snatch her soon enough.

He did not have long to lurk
before Chloe began her work
driving her sheep to the spring
leaving Daphnis behind spreading
green leaves for his goats. But
her dogs were quick to sniff out
Dorco sweating in the bracken;
they instantly had his scent,
and began to snap and snarl
incensed by his wolf smell
as he cringed in the dirt
unable to escape unhurt.

They bit him fiercely. Yet,
fearing exposure and that
he would be greatly shamed,
he tried to lie still as in a grave
and hid himself the best he could
in his pelt smeared with blood.
Chloe shouted out in fright
at she knew not what and cried
for Daphnis just as the hounds
tumbled his disguise and
rounded on Dorco with lips curled
so that he roared and wailed
begging Daphnis and Chloe
to save him. They called away
the dogs and, seeing his thighs
and arms bleed from the bites
of lethal teeth, they took him
to the Fountain and gently
washed his wounds. Chloe,
after chewing the bark of an elm,
soothed them softly with its balm.

Yet, still unread in the chapters
of love they thought the herder
masquerading in wolf skin
had merely been clowning
and made light of it. Treating
him with kindness and taking
his hand they said good-bye
and went their separate way
for they had much to do to
round up their goats and ewes
before it grew late in the day,
since the herds were still afraid
of the 'wolf' and the dogs' fierce
barks and snarls. Some had raced
amok among the ragged crags,

others to the cliffs in a zigzag
down to the shore even though
they were trained to the voice,
to the slap of clapped hands
and the pipe's soothing sounds.
But in time weaned off their fear
they returned to their fields.

That night Daphnis and Chloe
slept the sleep of sated babies
finding fatigue to be a threat
to the straight aisle of love; yet
as soon as the morning came
their emotions fizzed again,
though joy at seeing each other
was tempered with the fear
that fate could part them soon
and they knew not what to do.
All they saw was that kisses
had endangered Daphnis
and day-dreaming Chloe
in that mazy month of May.

Time winged by. Spring done,
the summer gone and autumn
flaring with ripened fruit,
the fields filled with wheat,
kindling of crickets chirruping
in bursting orchards, hopping
to the bleat of settled sheep.
You would think the streams
sang on their unhurried way,
imagine pine breezes to play
while the cattle, as if laid low
with love, slept in the meadows.
Then the vain unveiling Sun
without shame goaded every one
to frolic and rollick in undress.

All of which inflamed Daphnis
so that he went to the pools
and slow brooks to stay cool
and drink of their limpid pearls
to quench his fire for his girl;
whereas Chloe milked her herd,
curdled and kneaded the curd
into small round cheeses
fending off the prying flies.
Then she washed herself and braided
pine needles around her head;
she wrapped herself in hides,
and churning milk with wine
made a syllabub for them both.
Later knowing noon to approach
they teased and mesmerised
each other with widening eyes.
As she watched Daphnis she knew
she had fallen for a true,
brave, most handsome youth
and would swear on oath
she could find in him no flaw.
And for his part when he saw
her in her skins and pine headdress
ladling their syllabub he blessed
her as the fairest of nymphs
and playfully sought to trim
her coronet of slender boughs
around his own proud brow;
and when he had kissed it over
and over he would re-crown her
tenderly returning it to her head.
And when Daphnis bathed naked
Chloe would filch his chiton,
kiss it all over and put it on.
Sometimes they lobbed apples
at one another and dabbled

with each other's hair, dressing
it in trammels and tresses.
Chloe likened Daphnis's hair
to the myrtle since it flared
black, and because Chloe's face
was shiny and flushed Daphnis
likened it to the choicest apple.
He also allowed her to pootle
on his pipe; but whenever she
began to blow he would free
it from her lips and feather
it over his own to teach her;
by means of such a specious
ploy any ardent boy could kiss
his girl whenever he liked
at one remove from his pipe.

Once, playing a tune at midday,
the herds lying in the shade
Chloe fell into an easy sleep
and seeing this, Daphnis sheathed
his pipe and without shame or
fear was bold enough to pore
over her every limb with desire
eulogising softly to the air:

What prized eyes are these
that sleep? How sweetly breathes
her careless mouth! The fragrance
of apple blossom or meadow grass
could never compete with
hers yet I fear to kiss her lips.
Her loveliness pricks my heart.
But hush! Lest I wake her! Quiet,
you prattling grasshoppers;
your susurrus may arouse her
as might those goats' groans
with their angry clash of horns!

Foxes and fierce wolves, come!
Drag them away to their doom!

And during his quiet rhetoric
a swallow dropped a cricket
into Chloe's bosom where it
sought sanctuary and pricked
her from her sleep. She screamed.
Then spotting a bird flying near
and hearing Daphnis laugh
at her fright she checked herself
unfusing her drowsy eyes
while the cricket sang praises
to her warm soothing skin.
Poor Chloe screamed again
and Daphnis could neither cup
his laughter, nor pass up
a chance to dive his hand into
a virgin's breasts and rescue
the cricket which still crooned
in his clench. But then, when
she saw it, she had compassion
and took it back into her bosom.

Something else that she loved
was the call of the stock-dove
cooing from a nearby grove,
and Chloe wanted to know
the purpose of the bird's call.
So Daphnis told her a tale
herders had told him:

The bird
was once a beautiful maid
like you, and in the sleepwalk
of her youth she kept her flocks
as you do yours. She was skilful
in music, her herds were quelled

by voice and pipe and needed
no coaxing from the crook. She'd
sit beneath a tree in leaf
weaving a coronet of leaves
singing of Pan and his sorrows,
and her cows would never go
far from her.
                    A young man,
also a peasant but handsome
and musical, kept a herd
close by. Chancing as it were
to imitate her melody and tone
in a register high for a man
but dulcet for a maid, he lured
her eight best cows to his herd.
She took it badly that her flock
had dwindled, and was sick
to think his siren song charmed
better than hers becalmed.
So she beseeched the gods
to change her into a bird,
and they made a dove of her
to fly forever over pasture;
yet still you hear her complain
demanding her cows back again.

Such trifles and treats as these
made for a summer frieze.
But in the following year
and the grape harvest cleared
some Tyrrhenian pirates
crewing a Carian boat
sailed slyly to their shores
armed with bucklers and swords
and planned to plunder, ransack
and take away the pick
of all that came their way:

wines, great stores of grain,
the best honeycombs. They
rustled Dorco's oxen and they
even captured Daphnis
as he ambled by the sea;
but not Chloe, who was late
that day being somewhat distrait
and had only just driven her stock
out from Dryas's paddock.

When the pirates realised that
Daphnis was a clever catch
worth more than all their plunder,
they lingered no longer
in the fields among the herds
but hauled him howling aboard.
Not knowing what to do, he
cried loud and long for Chloe
who, unaware, was already
herding her sheep with a sturdy
new pipe for her Daphnis
as the pirates pulled away quickly
from the shore out to sea. So,
Chloe, seeing his goats
scattered and hearing him call
her loudly from the far shore
left her own flock and sped
lightning-fast to Dorco for help.
But Dorco had been treated
cruelly by the raiders and she
found him on the ground
blood pouring from a wound.
Yet seeing Chloe his old desire
pricked him and he told her:

I will soon die. Those pox-
ridden pirates took me for an ox

as I fought to save my drove.
But you must save your love
and in their unsparing ruin
avenge me on those villains.
I've trained my herd to heed
this pipe and obey its reed
even though they graze far away.
Come, take the pipe and play
the tune I taught your boy
and I know he taught you.
Trust in this pipe, Chloe,
and its solid supremacy
over all other herds. For this,
my dear, I ask only a kiss
while I still breathe. When I
am dead then you may cry
for me, and if you see another
on these hills with my herd
remember Dorco.
And so
with a kiss she released his soul.

Then, picking up the pipe,
wetting and pursing her lips
she began to blow as loud
as she could, and the cows
on the ship, restive, instantly
responded to the melody.
With baleful bellowing
they stampeded and flung
themselves into the sea,
and so fiercely did they flee
that the ship listed, canted,
took on heavy water and sank
with all hands. The pirates
in arms, chain mail corselets
and stoutly booted to the thighs

had little chance to survive
unlike Daphnis, always barefoot
since island summer grass is hot.
Though uncertain how to swim
having bathed only in streams
he threw off his ragged chiton
and coached by compulsion
thrashed about among the herd
holding a horn in each hand.
Unharmed he was borne ashore
as though a mighty charioteer.
And thus Daphnis was spared
from shipwreck and ashore
once more he found Chloe both
laughing and crying, and folded
her in his arms, puzzling how
she had saved him with the cows.
So she brightened and chirped
how she ran to Dorco for help,
how the cows knew to heed
the pitch of the pipe, how she'd
played his runic tune but that
dear Dorco was dead; yet
ashamed she omitted his kiss.
And in gratitude they blessed
their generous saviour and so
mournfully buried Dorco
with all the rites and sacraments
of the Elysian Ancients.

Thrice they blessed his soul
and built a barrow of soil
over his body. On his grave
they planted fragrant votives:
shrubs and perennial flowers,
and vowed aloud to offer
him each year their first fruit.
They also anointed the spot

with libations of milk, squeezed
over his grave only the purest
bunches of grapes, and then,
with tearful eyes, broke many
a herder's pipe in his name.
Cows and oxen also came
to bellow and low echoing
mourners in crestfallen tones.
Even the goats seemed to moan
at the loss of their guardian.

And when the funeral ended
Chloe took Daphnis by the hand
to the Nymphs' Cave where,
bared, they washed one another
even though her flawless skin
wanted neither water nor lanolin;
then, done with that, they chose
flowers to crown the statues
and hung Dorco's epic pipe
as a relic for his worship.

Later, they looked around
for their sheep and goats and found
that they neither grazed not bleated
but lay in silence as if defeated,
missing both Daphnis and Chloe
who'd been away all that day.
But when their stock saw
and heard them call their torpor
left them and they instantly rose
to purpose and began to graze
bleating and leaping easy
in their loyal drovers' keep.

Yet among them Daphnis
was unable to settle since

he had seen Chloe naked,
honeyed, tender, scented
and more lovely than Venus
in all her sensuousness.
His heart beat as if energised
by stimulants which induced
the ache of both love and death
resulting in shallow breaths
as if someone gave him chase;
yet at other times as if in a race
he could barely catch his wind.
It seemed to him that a pond
was more perilous than the sea,
as though it was yet likely
he would be recaptured by pirates,
for he was still a rustic whippet,
a puppy lost in the dense groves
and baffling labyrinths of love.

Second Canto

The autumn came suntanned,
and the vineyard crop to hand,
gleaners gathered its yield
like honeybees around orchids.
Some mended wine presses,
scoured tuns, casks, cruses
while others made baskets,
panniers, skeps or fetched
grabs and billhooks to reap
the highest bunches of grapes.
One would search the scree
for quartz to grind grape seed
while another turned a stang
of dry smooth wood by hand
to hod a must-sack in the night
carried in by lantern light.

And so Daphnis and Chloe
forsook their flocks to go
and hurry in the harvest.
Daphnis, a slave to the press,
tipped grapes from his skep,
trampled them barefoot
and tunned the juice in butts.
As for Chloe she limbed meat
for the harvesters, serving them
lees wine diluted to the brim
with fountain water; and when
she had indulged them she went
to gather grapes from the vines,
since on Lesbos at that time
their leaves dragged on the soil

like writhing ivy so that a boy
with racing hands could reach
them easily to release a bunch.

And as was usual in autumn
when the peasant women came in
from neighbouring fields seduced
by the feast day of Dionysus
they craved after Daphnis
and compared him to the god.
Often some strapping lass would
ensnare him for a saucy kiss,
and more and more such lusting
flustered the blushing boy, stung
him afire but made Chloe vexed.
Yet some, pounding in the press,
prized her too, sang her praises
as though she were a goddess;
like drunken Satyrs steeped in lust
they pined to be in her trust
at which she was quietly pleased
though jealousy daggered Daphnis.
Yet both wished the feasting done
and to return soon to the downs;
to swap these bacchanals
for a pipe and the lowing of cattle.

And with the grapes gleaned
and pressed and the wine tunned
their help was no longer needed
so they returned to the fields
to drive their flocks once more.
There, in good heart they adored
and revered the Nymphs, offering
first clusters of their gatherings;
and they were never remiss
as they passed by the Nymphs

in taking their food into the Cave
with rare reverential love.
When at home they blessed them,
praying for their protection
forever offering oblations:
a flower, an apple, an apron
teeming with leaves, or milk
so that for their piety and vigil
they met with no meagre merit
and favour from the Nymphs.
As free as mountain rills
they skipped, reeled and trilled
each piping to their flocks.

One day, during their frolics
an old man approached clothed
in a jerkin of skins, hose,
a mantle and carbatine shoes;
on his back hung a well-used
ragged haversack, and he settled
beside them to tell this tale:

I am that old Philetas
who often sang for the Nymphs
and played to the great god Pan
having led gargantuan
herds by my music alone;
and I am here to make known
what I have seen and heard.
I have a garden, cleared
and planted by these hands
after I gave up my herds
because of old age; it is a joy
to cultivate, trim and hoe;
there are fruits and flowers
for every season of the year.
In the spring are rambling roses,
lilies, hyacinths and rows

of violets of every colour;
in the summer – poppies, pears
and all the cultivars of apple;
the autumn trees teem full
of pomegranates, lemons,
oranges, myrtles and melons.
Every morning on the wind
birds come to feed and sing
in my lush, shaded glen
flushed by a triple fountain.

Yesterday after midday
while I lay there a boy
appeared in the pomegranate
and myrtle orchard with fruit
in his hands, white as hoar
blazing with rays of fire,
pure and radiant as if he came
fresh clean from a fountain.
He was naked and alone
and rioted in the groves
pulling and snapping stems
as if in his own garden.
I was afraid lest this minx
with his impish high jinks
in my grove might quickly
destroy the fruit and trees.
But he was slick and swift
and easily gave me the slip,
sometimes under the roses
sometimes in the poppies
like a scurrying quail chick.
I've often had to do with
goat kids and skittish calves
harrying me to my grave
but his silky elusiveness
was entirely something else.

Worn out, being an old cove,
shorn up by my staff, though
alert lest he ran off, I asked
whose neighbour's rascal
he was and why he raided
another man's orchard.
But he answered not a word
and coming nearer chortled
most becomingly; he pitched
at me myrtle berries which
entranced, how I know not
so that my rage was spent.
So I asked him to draw near,
no need to fear, and assured
him that he may not only take
the apples and pomegranates
but also pick the finest fruit
and flowers whenever it suited
him if he would grant me a kiss.
But the boy laughed, hissed
just like a storming swan,
swallow, nightingale or robin
and metamorphosed into
an old man like me. 'You!'
he said. 'It would be no bother
to give you a kiss, since there
would be more in it for me
than someone no longer sappy
like you. But consider – lust
always rusts in decrepitude
and old age will slow you;
it will be futile to pursue
me after I've darted you a kiss.
I cannot be out-raced
by hawk, eagle or swifter bird.
You can see I am not that child
I seemed to be, but am older

even than Sisyphus's boulder.
I knew you as a young ruffian
who kept his herd in a far fen.
I hovered close when you sang
under rich beech trees and
played your pipe for Amaryllis.
You never saw me but I was
there beside the lass you loved.
It was I who blessed your grove
so that you had contented sons
and means. And now unseen
I am Daphnis's champion;
and when I have bonded
the lovers each day I withdraw
into your garden with the dew,
and shower in your flowers,
dry myself under your bowers
which is why your roses,
violets, lilies and poppies
– all your flora never fade
because they are watered
by my washing. Look about
and see whether underfoot
one stem or twiglet lies split,
whether any of your fruits
have dropped or any flower
lies lopped; look, do your
fountains splutter with slime?
You are favoured in your decline!'

Reverting to a boy again he
sprang among the myrtle trees
and like a nightingale bounced
from leafy branch and bough
atop the tallest tree.
I saw his wings and between
them at his back a short bow

and with it two tiny arrows,
but have not seen him since.
So, if I am not grey and wise
in vain, you are both destined
to love since Eros is your friend.

Though sunlit with delight
Daphnis and Chloe thought it
to be but an island legend
not a true narrative and begged:
Who is Eros? A boy, a bird?
to which Philetas replied:

Eros is a fine young god
with wings, greatly enamoured
of youth and beauty. He strives
for compassion in our lives.
Jove's might is less immense.
He governs the elements,
steers the stars, domineers
even the other gods, his peers;
and your sheep and goats
which you think you host
he too has dominion there.
Flowers form by his labour,
plants and poems. Through
him rivers rise, winds too.
I have known a lovesick cow
bellowing in the meadow
bolt as if goaded by a prod;
a bewitched billy too, hard
on a maiden goat's tail
pine after her through dales,
wild trails and grassy groves.
I myself when young and in love
with Amaryllis, often forgot
to dine and drink. At night

love-weary I could not sleep,
my sad panting heart leapt,
my body writhed with cold.
How often have I cried
as if beaten black and blue,
lain low in a slough as though
buried among the dead; dived
into rivers as if on fire
and called on Pan to rescue
me since he too had pursued
the unrequited love of Pitys.
I blessed Echo so that thrice
she called out 'Amaryllis';
and I broke my pipes because,
though they always quelled
my herd, heeling them to my will –
they would not drive her to me.
For there is no known remedy
for love, no potion, no drink
no antidote; only kisses
while naked in each other's arms.

Thus Philetas quelled their qualms
and his wide-eyed listeners brought
him cheeses and a young goat;
then he blessed them and left.

Alone, their minds adrift
in this knowledge they began
to ponder Philetas's tuition,
weighing a lover's great love
against sensibilities suffered:
how wooers moped and grieved
they in themselves perceived.
Despairing they became careless
in their chores, could not rest
longing for the light of day,

were feverish even in the spray
of fountains and cool of streams
and wanted nothing but to be
with each other – this one idea
seeing them through each day.
For surely they were in love
and yet knew little thereof.

Philetas did not lie one mote
for they knew without doubt
that the boy in the garden,
also spotted by their fathers
Lamo and Dryas, was the one
who aroused them unseen
in the meadows and fields.
But how to catch him? He'd
slip their grip being lithe.
And how would they even fly
after him since he had wings?
Should they implore the Nymphs,
for did not Pan help Philetas
when he was mad for Amaryllis?
So they set about the cures
Philetas had told them before
he left: kissing, embalmed
tightly in each other's arms.

Yet for them it was a game
– a thrilling daily pastime.
And each day, their flocks
driven from the paddocks
to the fields, they ran to kiss
with a fierce impatience
they had never known before.
And yet to venture as far
as to lie together unclothed
which Philetas had extolled

they dared not be so brazen
since for a young maiden
and a goatherd it was a cure
too far. And so, as before
they suffered sleepless nights
reliving their rapture despite
rueing all they might miss,
making sense of it like this:

We kiss and love doing it;
we hug and cuddle too but
that doesn't seem enough.
So to lie together nude
seems the only remaining cure
for love. We must therefore
try it, for perhaps somehow
it'll be, though hard to see how,
more delicious than a kiss.

And since such thoughts leased
their amorous dreams at night
they enacted what they dare not
do for real: that is to undress
and then lovingly caress.
So that come the morning as if
inspired by some dream spirit
they rose to drive their herds
with fire and fury to the fields,
and ran to kiss inspired by
each other's love-sick smiles.
Making love this way they did,
but to lie naked not one bit
since because Chloe was timid
Daphnis dare not hint at it.
Then one day by artless luck
sitting together on the trunk
of an old oak tree rehearsing

the finesse of their kissing
steeped in ravenous desire,
a mutual impulse inspired
their arms to kite and knit,
their lips to cling like limpets.
And when he hugged her
with a desperate desire
which she traded with fire
he collapsed on top of her,
so that reliving their dreams
they lay there a long time
tight together perplexed
by what they should do next
to express their great passion.
And so the day passed in vain
and they parted after herding
their flocks home, cursing
the coming of loveless night.
Perhaps it was only right
and auspicious since calamity
was about to rout their fields.

The young men of Methymna
musing how to pass the time
of the wine harvest holiday
fixed on heroics far away,
and launching a small boat
made their manservants row
to the farmlands of Mitylene,
for its coast had many lagoons,
deep coves and safe harbours,
stately buildings with stairs,
spars, laid gardens and groves
favouring them where they roved.

Their boat moored in a bay
they engaged in much horseplay

but causing no harm nor mishap:
they also fished from outcrops
or with hounds harried hard
startled hares in the vineyards.
At other times they went fowling
for wild geese, mallards, lapwings,
marsh birds and by such sport
exercised their hungry jaws.

If they needed further victuals
they were generous to the locals
though little was actually wanted
other than bread, wine and a bed
for it was their custom
not to sleep aboard in Autumn
but to have their boat moored
in case of a surprise storm.

One such wild night a rustic,
wanting rope to haul a rock
for grinding grape stones
in the winter (his own
having snapped) sneaked down
to their boat's berth, found
it bereft of crew, undid
the holding hawser and stole it
for his own hit-nail ends.
At sunrise its crewmen
searched for the rope but no one
confessed to its theft, and when
they had berated their hosts
for their part in its loss
they sailed on several leagues
arriving at the very fields
grazed by Chloe and Daphnis,
which looked a likely place
for the hunting of wild hare.

For want of a rope to moor
the boat they made bindings
of long green willow twigs
and with them secured it tight
to the shore so they might
safely stow aboard their oars and
prime their dogs to hunt the land.
Jaw and jowl they howled
and bolted far barking loud
goading the goats to the sea
who, finding nothing to eat,
gnawed the bindings to pieces
just as a mountain breeze
whipped up the waves to set
the untethered boat afloat
and carry it out to sea.
Some of the crew, seeing
it go, flew to the shore
while the dogs were recalled,
and such a rumpus erupted
that all the farmers abruptly
stopped work near the coast.
But to no avail, all was lost.
Their boat was very swiftly
with an evil inevitability
whisked away to the horizon.
And so the Methymnians
incensed at their reverse
scoured for any goatherd
and falling on Daphnis
beat him, tore his tunic
and bound him like straw.
Badly bruised he roared
for his countrymen
to come to his salvation.
Hewn from the rugged rock

of island pastoral stock
they bristled, demanded
to know what had happened
and sued for a fair hearing.
Philetas chose to oversee
the debate as its arbiter
being the oldest, most popular
for dispensing justice
in all village disputes.

The Methymnians began
accusing poor Daphnis in
plain language archly hinged
at a simple rustic judge:

We came to hunt these fields,
and moored our boat with green
sallow tethers. As our pack
was hunting, the goats dashed
from the mountains to the sea,
worried the bindings to pieces
and cast our boat free. There!
See her shimmer on the water
laden with our choice rich ware
lost to us now with fine fieldwear,
rare dog harnesses and
enough silver to buy this land.
In recompense it is only fit
we take this herder captive
seeing how he let his goats
feed freely around our boat.

But Daphnis, his bones sore,
spotting Chloe standing near
set their charge at nought
and countered with this retort:

I am a good herdsman;
no one in these lowlands
has ever blamed me for
allowing a kid or goat
to ruin their great gardens
or dine on their fertile vines.
Yet these wild vile hunters
have unruly hounds. Their
furious coursing, their baying
wolf-like panicked my kids
and goats, chased them in
the vales from mountains
to coast. They ate the bindings
only because there was nothing
else on the beach to eat –
neither shrub, herb nor tree.
It was the wind in the waves
which took their boat away;
the storm at sea is guilty,
not my goats. Anyway with rich
clothes, collars, apparel
and silver aboard I marvel
that they used weak willows
to moor her and not hawsers!

Daphnis began to whimper
to win the judge over
so that good Philetas sued
Pan and the Nymphs to rule
that Daphnis and his herd
had done nothing wretched.
It was the sea and the wind
which merited reprimand.
Yet Philetas's verdict
wholly failed to convince
the Methymnians who began
to shackle Daphnis again.

So the villagers waged war
like mad snapping jackdaws
bustling him away in haste
with clubs. Then they chased
the blackguards from the bay.

Withdrawn far from the melee
Chloe was free to take Daphnis
to the fountain of the Nymphs
to wash his wounded face
and help him to convalesce
after his escape with cheese
and bread from her valise.
More than ever she kissed
him in her distress because
he had almost been killed. Yet
their troubles did not abate
for the soft-bellied sons
of Methymna, their presumption
wounded, travelled back home
in misery, and abjectly forlorn
before their council urged
that their reverse be avenged;
but they petalled their version
lest they should be scorned
as lumpkins. They charged
the Mitylenians with pillage
and unprovoked acts of war.
Their people, seeing their scars
and trusting their patrician word
swiftly accepted their absurd
lies and voted to even the score.
And short of declaring war
they commanded Bryaxes
their great general to attack
the coastline of Mitylene
with a fleet of ten triremes

since winter being close
they thought it dangerous
to send a greater squadron.

With high tide opportune
the general put out to sea
and soon came to Mitylene.
He invaded its islands,
ravaging and sacking the land,
its flocks, corn and wine,
(all the harvest now being in)
and terrifying the working poor.
They also pounced on the pasture
grazed by Chloe and Daphnis
as if swooping from the heavens
and razed all they came across.

But at that time Daphnis was
not with his herd but had left
for a wood to bind up leaves
for winter fodder; and so
looking down from a plateau
stun-shocked by the attack
he hid in an old hollow oak.
Yet Chloe was with her herd
and fled from the invaders
to the Nymphs' Cave begging
them to spare her and her kin
in the name of the Goddesses.
It was to no avail; her aggressors
not only mocked and abused
the Nymphs' holy statues
but stampeded her sheep far
from the Cave and captured her
as if she were a beast of burden.
And with their boats richly laden
they rowed back to their lands
since there was no serving wind.

Running from the high fields
Daphnis found neither sheep,
goats nor his Chloe; only
her silent pipe and misery.
In tears, his sad heart torn,
he ran down to the shore
where Chloe used to stray
hoping to find her in the bay;
and not seeing her, he ran
to the Cave where she hid
before her capture. Prostrate
before them he berated
the Nymphs for her ill-use:

It was from your statues
that Chloe was abducted
and ravished! How could you
bear to see it. For you
she made garlands. To you
every morning she sacrificed
the first milk, her pipe
hangs here as a devotion.
No wolf has ever taken
one goat from me, yet this foe
takes our flocks as well as Chloe,
my one true friend in the world.
They will butcher our herds
and Chloe will die in their city.
How can I face our families!
I am ruined, I have no trade,
no flock of goats to feed.
I am no longer a goatherd.
I lie here disfavoured
in grief expecting to die
in any attempt to free Chloe.
And are you, dear Chloe, also

as desperate as I? Do you
still remember our fields,
the beach, the Nymphs and me?
Do you still care for your ewes
those they pillaged with you?

And as he choked on their lot
fatigue overtook him and rocked
him to sleep so that the Nymphs
came to him in a dream: three
beautiful women, shoeless
and with easy hair dressed
like their statues. At first
they pitied what he had lost
then to hearten him said:

Do not blame us; we paid
greater care to Chloe's fate
than you, her lover; we wait
on her as our dependant
as if we were her parents.
Chloe does not belong to
the land, neither to Lamo,
nor to his sheep. Have peace!
We have plotted her release:
she will not live as a slave
in Methymnia, a prey to knaves.
We've begged the great god Pan,
whose statue is under that pine
where you've been remiss
with your votives of flowers,
to restore Chloe to our care.
For Pan is used to warfare
either in city or forest pines
and the Methymnians will find
him to be a murderous foe.
Mourn and moon no more. Go

to wretched Lamo and Myrtle
who think you also in shackles.
For it is certain Chloe
will come to you tomorrow
with her sheep and your goats,
and you will herd and blow
your pipes together as before.
Let love take care of all.

After the dream had passed
he arose feeling blessed
though still with tearful eyes,
and vowed to the statues
to sacrifice his best beast if
Chloe were returned safely.
He rushed to the sacred pine
hallowed by the statue of Pan
with cloven hooves, horns and
a proud pipe in one hand,
in the other a prancing goat,
and praised him, begging that
he restore Chloe in one piece.
Then, ceasing to keen and weep
he found his fardel of boughs
in the wood and ran down
to the cottage to comfort Lamo,
making him easy once more.
There he refreshed himself
with meat and wine and slept
after more tears and prayers
willing the Nymphs to reappear
but wishing the night gone
too and the morning to come
early bringing Chloe to his side.
But it was a long rare night
bringing with it such marvels!

The Methymnian general,
having sailed some few leagues,
wished to refresh his fatigued
sea-sick soldiers after their
avenging ravaging raids.
Thus, off a natural mole
(a crescent moon-shaped wall
which spoiled the sea's sport)
they moored safer than in port.
There he dropped anchor to let
his men carouse freely and set
about feasting with dance
secure from attack by land.

But later at night in their revels
they saw the shore bedevilled
by fire and in their ears roared
the clatter of a thousand oars
as though a great navy loomed
close. Obeying a call-to-arms,
they thought themselves attacked
imagining the blooded features
of dying men, and each one
believed himself embroiled in
a night battle even though
they could see neither ships nor foe.

The morning's nightmares
were even more bizarre
when each goat's horns suddenly
sprouted berry-laden ivy
while Chloe's sheep were heard
to howl like wolves in a wood.
She herself queened pivotal
among them with pine needles
crowning her brow. In the sea
were wonders, monstrosities

and rare phenomena; the more
they strove to weigh anchor
the firmer they stuck in bedrock.
Their lowered oars cracked
on impact and leaping dolphins
ripped the boats with their fins,
their tails slicing the hulks' ribs.
Then, from a high crag drifting
over the promontory cape
the appalling sound of a pipe
was heard, not honeyed but like
a terrible trumpet, grimly hostile
causing each man to curse
an enemy he could not see.
How they wanted night again
so that a truce might reign.
Yet the source of these phantoms
could easily have been fathomed
by wise men since the spectres
and grisly sounds were vested
in Pan, though for what reason
they had absolutely no notion
since his statue stood unruined.

Then, the general in his cabin
was plunged into a deep sleep
and Pan damned him in a dream:

Oh, you most cruel dissolute
of mortals! What made you
so mad as to do the things
you did? You've not only
filled these fields with war,
which are to me so dear,
but you have also rustled
those sheep and goat herds
in my special care and keep.

You have dared to kidnap
from the altar of the Nymphs
a maid of whom Eros himself
will write her story. Nor did you
sacrifice at my sacred statue
though you passed my image.
For this you will never voyage
to Methymnia again or sail
from here with your spoils,
nor escape my perilous pipe
but will drown without hope
unless you quickly restore
Chloe to the Nymphs with all
her flocks. Awake therefore
and send the maiden ashore
with her sheep and goats,
and I will steer you home,
and guide her to her lands.

Bryaxis woke from his trance
and called together the captains
of all the boats to explain
that Chloe must be found
among the captives. Crowned
with pine and thus stark visible
they brought her to the general
who, recalling from his dream
that pines are an emblem
of distinction, had Chloe
carried to land in ceremony.

And once she was ashore
Pan's pipe played once more
no longer strident or dire
but a more pleasing pastoral air
one that was often used to lead
herds to feed in the fields.

The sheep too were rescued;
not one fell overboard, hooved
though they were; the goats too
being surefooted and used
to drunken craggy cliff sides.
And the whole flock clustered
round Chloe as if in dance
skipping and bleating to express
their unbounded joy and love.
Yet the animals in the other
herds made no attempt to leave
but remained on board enslaved
as if the pipe had no power.

As witness to these wonders
the Methymnians praised Pan.
But one more aberration
was seen on that rarest of days –
before anchors could be weighed
the boats were swept to sea,
their flag ship shown the way
by a mighty diving dolphin,
while inland the dulcet fine
playing of a pipe dispersed
the flocks of the shepherdess;
yet no one saw the piper
or knew from where he piped.

At grazing time after midday
Daphnis, fixing on Chloe
from his high plateau meadow
shadowing her flock, crowed:
O Nymphs! O blessed Pan!
and panted down to the plains
to pour himself into her embrace
collapsing them into the grass.
They kissed without restraint

where they fell and then went
holding hands happily
to their favoured beech tree.
There, cradled in its shade,
he asked how she had evaded
such callous captivity?
So Chloe began her story:
how the ivy had grown
full-berried on goat horns,
sheep had bayed like wolves,
and how a pine crown wreathed
her head and all the earth
seemed to burn; of the unearthly
rackets and clashes heard
out at sea; the fierce weird
pipe's mysterious melody
from the craggy promontory –
first bellicose, then mouse-like;
of the spectres of the night;
and how she was kidnapped
and not knowing her way back
had only the sweet music
of the pipe, spectral, Delphic,
for her guide and companion.

Daphnis then told of his vision
involving the Nymphs and Pan
and what he had heard and seen;
how, when he had expected
to die he was protected
and preserved by the agency
and patience of the Nymphs.

Then he asked her to invite
Dryas and Lamo to a sacrifice
and bring everything necessary
for worshipping the Nymphs

and Pan. Meanwhile, he caught
the best of his she-goats,
titivated it with ivy
(just like their enemy had seen
on their boats), poured milk
on its festooned horns and killed
it in the name of the Nymphs.
Then he racked the flayed skin,
consecrated it and from there on
it became an object of devotion.

When she returned with their folk
he lit a fire and roasted the goat
offering the choicest parts
to the gods; and filling a patera
with wine he made a libation;
then, having with care laid down
several beds of green leaves
they gave themselves leave
to feast and drink to the roof,
while ever vigilant for wolves.
They sang dirges and hymns
of reverence to the Nymphs,
and lay all night under the sky,
rising with the dawn to glorify
the great god Pan's miracles
by leading the herd's finest male,
crowned with pine garlands,
to his statue; there they rained
wine upon its head with
eulogies and panegyrics
before sacrificing it to their
god, their generous saviour.
Its dressed roasted meat
was laid on layers of leaves.
They pegged out the hide
with its horns onto the Pine

near the statue and dedicated
it to their Arcadian god
offering him the first carving.
Daphnis played and Chloe sang
and with these rites at an end
they sat to feast yet again.

At a late hour the herdsman,
Philetas, approached them
bringing with him garlands
and grapes to honour Pan.
His youngest son, Tityrus –
florid of face and with fierce
eyes, leapt and romped like
a frisky kid goat at his side.
Welcomed by the throng
recognising his standing
they rose as one to crown
the sacred statue of Pan
with intricate wreaths, bunches
of ripe grapes and pine branches.
Then they invited old Philetas
and Tityrus to be their guests.
As old men are wont to crow
about their fearless bravado
they began to trade stories
swelling their former glories
while protecting their flocks;
how often they had driven off
countless attacks and invasions
of pirates, rustlers and brigands.
One bragged that he had slain
the largest wolf on the plains;
another that he was second
only to Pan and already a legend
for playing his pipe with finesse.
That was old Philetas no less.

Therefore Daphnis and Chloe
spun a web of flattery
to coax him into unveiling
his art of pipe playing,
so he would play at Pan's feast
whom they knew he loved best.
Philetas agreed and though age
denied him breath he obliged
himself to use Daphnis's pipe;
yet it miscarried so fine
a skill as his, being more suited
to a tyro piper instead.
So he dispatched Tityrus
for his own pipe, their house
being but ten furlongs distant.
The boy free of his raiments
raced as fast as a hind
while Lamo offered to recite
the Pipe's Tale which a hireling
from Sicily had once told him:

how the pipe was once
no instrument but a beauteous
maiden with a honeyed
melodious voice who herded
goats, playing and singing
with the sacred Nymphs.
One day tending her herd
in this way Pan came to her
vowing her goats would twin
each year if she lay with him.
But the maid Syrinx in scorn
of his love refused to take one
who was neither goat nor man
to her heart. Yet Pan pestered
her, proposing to take her
by force. At first she escaped

but, wearying swiftly, slipped
into a reed bed only to sink
in the fen and disappear within.
In fury Pan rushed into the reeds
but not finding her there
bound several quills together,
each of different length because
their love was discrepant. Thus
Syrinx, a virgin without vice,
became his own personal pipe.

After Lamo had told his tale
Philetas praised it as an idyll
far sweeter than any song.
Then Tityrus returned along
with his father's fine pipe,
its reeds sealed side by side
in staggered size with wax
and emblazoned in bronze
so brilliant that any one
would think it belonged to Pan.

Philetas made himself easy
on a bench, blew each reed
to hear if it pitched true,
and finding them all in tune
played a loud and lusty air
pitch-tone perfect on the ear.
Yet little by little he honed
a softer mellower tune,
and trilling with infinite skill
flaunted airs more suitable
for cows, goats and sheep.
For ewes his pitch was sweet
and low, for cattle much more
strident, and shrill and razor
for the goats. In the summer

that one pipe outperformed
those of all the other droves
their herders sitting attentive
silently listening with envy,
but charmed by its music.

Next Dryas rose to ask for
a Dionysiac or Bacchic air
and as one they all began
to dance the Epilenion,
the ballet of the winepresses
loosely based on the harvest:
the garnering of the grapes,
the carrying of the skeps,
crushing fruit under foot,
tunning the wine into butts
and the orgic carousing
of the must. All these things
he represented so precisely,
so tightly did his mime fit,
that the vines, grapes, must
and butts became real just
as if its wine could be drunk.

When the dancing ceased
the tired old man kissed
both Chloe and Daphnis,
and they then rose quickly
to act out Lamo's story –
Pan portrayed by Daphnis
and Chloe miming Syrinx.
He pleaded and teased to try
to win her but she was shy,
laughing at his love. She fled
and Daphnis chased to head
her off, running on tip-toes
to imitate Pan's hooves.

For her part Chloe enacted
Syrinx's plight, her flight
to the wood and its swamp.
Then Daphnis, picking up
Philetas's great pipe, played
a doleful dirge, spraying
quavers of love to persuade
her to relent with a serenade;
he wooed her from the wood
with all the passion he could.
And Philetas, overcome
with joy and admiration,
could not still his enthusiasm.
Kissing Daphnis he gave him
his great pipe with orders
to will it to a successor
like himself, and Daphnis then
pledging his own pipe to Pan
hung it on the divine Pine tree.
Then, kissing the fair Chloe
as if she had genuinely come
from the fen, he drove home
his herd, piping down the track.

Chloe followed his flock's
merry music, their goats
and sheep mingling because
they strolled holding hands.
And they talked till the end
of the day; then vowed to turn
their flocks out at early dawn.
This they did. As soon as
it was morning they arose
and went to the grazing fields
genuflecting at the effigies
of Pan and the holy Nymphs.
Later, under an oak still

in the modesty of early day
they heard Philetas play
and kissed and hugged
on the ground but shrugged
off doing more. Then they rose
to eat and drink wine soused
with milk, and feeling brave
agonised over their love
sealing it with an oath,
so that Daphnis approached
the holy Pine and swore to Pan
that he could not live alone
on Earth more than one day
without his Chloe. And Chloe
swore in the Nymphs' shrine
that she would live and die
with Daphnis. Yet a tiny doubt
caught in her parched throat
being so young, so that when
she came out from the shrine
she sought yet more assurance
from Daphnis saying this:

Pan is a wanton, wicked god
since he loved Pitys and wooed
Syrinx too. Besides, he never
ceases to seduce and pester
the Dryads and the Nymphs
under the apple trees.
Therefore, if you are untrue
to me he'll barely punish you
though you take as many maids
as reeds in his pipe. Make
this oath to me by your herd
and by that goat which nursed
you as her own – that you will
never forsake me while

I am faithful to you, and if
I am false and the Nymphs
abandon me, you yourself
must slay me like a wolf.

Daphnis swallowed hard
and in the guts of his herd
with one hand on a she-goat
and the other at a male's throat
he swore to love his Chloe
as she loved him; and that if
she ever preferred another
to him he would murder
this he-goat instead of her.
Chloe was as reassured
as any young innocent maid
might be, having been reared
with sheep and goat herds
on this island of shepherds.

Third Canto

When the Mitylenians heard
of the fleet's forays and raids,
the ravaging and pillage of loot
they felt it an affront too
grievous for grist, and in anger
raised arms against Methymna,
(five thousand horse soldiers,
three thousand targettiers)
and sent their general, Hippasus,
by land not daring to trust
the sea in storm. He ordered
the villages, farms and herds
to be spared as they passed over
the province, that not one door
be hammered hard (deeming
such violation in keeping
with mercenaries) and struck
for the city to take it by shock.

However, still miles away,
an enemy emissary
met them to parley and said
his people had been misled:
that it was their own gallants
who'd provoked the peasants
and herders of Mitylene; they
were the cause of this enmity;
that the Methymnians rued
this upstart lunatic feud
and Bryaxis' attack against
a neighbouring city state.
So these were their terms:

all slaves to be reclaimed
all plunder to be returned
and to trade by sea and land
in peace with their noble city.

Hippasus sent the emissary
on to Mitylene and made
his camp within ten stadia
of Methymna where he
awaited news from his city.
Within two days the legate
returned with a mandate
to reclaim all the pillage
and prisoners and march
home without further loss.
So Methymna sued for peace
prizing it more profitable
than war and this quarrel
between two city states
for several years abated.

Now came the winter freeze
which for Chloe and Daphnis
was much worse than any war.
Suddenly a rogue snowfall
veiled all trails and tracks
jailing them in their shacks.
Many streams and rivers froze
glistering like crystal quartz;
hedges and trees grew quills
and hillocks wore the frills
of springs and becks. No more
were herds driven to pasture,
nor did anyone call on another;
and at cock-crow each drover
lit his fire to flame brow-high.
Some spun raw flax or dyed

their clothes while others made
fake lures, bird nets and snares.
Each took every care to feed
their oxen and cows with reeds
in their stalls, goats and sheep
with hoarded oats and leaves
in their pens and folds, while
to fatten the hogs in their sties
they fed them swill and acorns.

But once their chores were done
the villagers and herders
were as busy as spiders
on a brimming web; they
would bustle to breakfast late
after long drunken nights so that
for them winter was in fact
a far more genial season
than spring, summer or autumn.
And yet Chloe and Daphnis
missed how they used to kiss
and embrace, and grieved how
their vows had been ploughed
under a sterile winter white.
Through long sad sleepless nights
they dreamily wanted nothing
more than to revisit the spring
in all its winged regeneration.

Neither did it please either one
to chance on the very satchel
which had carried their victuals
to the fields, and the syllabub cup
from which they'd both supped;
or if they happened to see
their pet pipe – that legacy
of a faithful friend. It was then

they asked the Nymphs and Pan
to summon the sun to shed
pieces of gold on their herds
that they might be released
from these fruitless miseries.

And therefore, praying alike,
they schemed to be reunited.
Yet poor Chloe had no one
to advise her and no plan,
for the old woman she took
to be her mother never forsook
her side, teaching her to card
wool, twirl spindles, spin yarn;
or else was always prattling
on about trifles or tattling
about her marriage. Daphnis,
however, with a ready wit
and more leisure, did conjure
one way he might see her.

In front of Dryas' hovel,
and from beneath it as well,
grew two tall myrtles linked
by lingering ivy so that with
its fierce busy-bodying among
the fecund branches, fronds
and plump clusters of berries
it made a natural arbour;
and for want of winter worms
ravening flights of birds would
raid it – blackbirds, redwings,
thrushes, doves and starlings.
He planned to catch them close
to Chloe's snowbound home.

Daphnis made his way there
with bait and lime-twig snares.

Lying some ten furlongs away
the drifts were deep and heavy
but woodland streams iced over
and savage Scythian snows are
no barrier to a lover's passion.
So, snow-caped, he came upon
the cottage and when he had
shook the ice from his back,
he set his snares under secreted
lime-twigs; then, shy-seated,
he thought only of his Chloe
as the birds flew into the ivy
pitching in a myriad ways.
All day they had him chasing,
snapping their necks, dressing
them for the table but no one
came from the cottage, no man
or woman, not so much as a hen
from the door; all were shut up
roosted cosy as in a coop.
Poor Daphnis was at a loss,
cold-perishing in the frost;
his bird plot had faltered
and now he needed shelter –
a reason to knock at the door.

He could say, he thought,
that he had come for fire wood,
but there was none to be had
ten furlongs around.
If I beg
for bread they'll see my bag
of cakes. I could say, a wolf
chased me but there's no proof
since there are no paw prints.
Having caught my birds, isn't
it more reasonable to go home?

Yet I must see Chloe, and so
how can I fashion favour
with her mother and father
while the house stays silent?
Not one of these expedients
is beyond suspicion. So
I give up. I'll see my Chloe
at the first peep of spring
since this how the Fates spin.

While such thinking racked
his mind he gathered his catch
to turn for home. But then,
as if Eros smiled on him,
serendipity struck while Dryas
was feasting. Meat, dressed
on a lavish table was allied
with copious craters of wine,
and suddenly a sheepdog
ran outside with a large leg
of tasty mutton. Dryas raved,
snatched his club and chased
the thief into the ivy arbour
where the young paramour
stood gathering up his birds.

Hail, lad! Dryas's words
heralded a warm embrace
as he led him to the house.
The lovers heard their hearts
beat again after being apart;
would have swooned had their
tightly leashed demeanours
not set them rigid as columns.
Yet Daphnis, despite reservations,
not only had a kiss from Chloe
but sat beside her in ecstasy

by the open fire and littered
the table with his catch of birds.
He told them of his boredom
caged an ice-age indoors;
how, needing sport and trade,
he had left to bait these birds
they could now see; how he
trapped them with his trickery
using lime-twigs and snares
as they pecked myrtle berries.

For this they praised Daphnis
as if he were Apollo no less
and bid Chloe serve the wine
which she did with a smile
for everyone except Daphnis;
he earned a sterner face
because he had deserted her.
Yet at last she did offer
him the kylix, kissing it,
sipping a little from its lip,
and he drank from it freely
to prolong her virtual kiss.

Dinner done, the table cleared
everyone began to revere
Lamo and Myrtle's marriage
like wine enriched with age;
and Daphnis too was pleased
to be praised in Chloe's eyes,
even the more so when asked
to tarry there until the next
day and help them sacrifice
to the god Bacchus. At once
he gave them his sack of cakes,
and his bird catch to be cooked
for supper. A fresh wine urn

was filled, the fire re-laid to burn
and they invited their guest
to dine. After another great feast
they told old tales and chanted
folk songs, then went to bed:
Chloe to her mother's, Daphnis
settling down with Dryas.
But nothing would appease poor
Chloe until she could see her
Daphnis again in the morning;
and Daphnis, also mooning,
consoled himself with amorous
fantasies lying next to Dryas,
and dreamed of her embrace
always burnished with a kiss.

Morning roped off a night frost
and the north wind reinforced
winter when they all roused,
and their high spirits ploughed
another day's loam. With pious
entreaties to Bacchus, Dryas
sacrificed a ram and the spit
was turned to roast its meat.
Nape made sacrificial bread
and Dryas fed the fire with wood
while the two lovers ventured
into the ivy-myrtle arbour.
Daphnis set yet more snares;
then they kissed without a pause
until they had need of air
and reviewed their love affair:

– *Chloe, I came for your sake.*
– *I know, Daphnis,* Chloe said.
– *It's because I longed for you*
  I slew these birds which flew;

wastrel though I am, love me.
– By the Nymphs I kneeled to
in the cave where once more
we will go when the ice thaws
I will always remember you.
– But the snow sticks like glue.
Sadly I fear I will melt first.
– Courage, Daphnis, the sun stirs.
– I would it burn like the fire
in my heart. You do but jeer.
– Never! By the goats you made
me swear on! Chloe replied.

Then, Nape called them back,
with yet more birds in his sack,
for the libation to Dionysus
before the saturnalias
with ivy crowning their heads.
But later, having sung ballads
to Jacchus and Euous, Daphnis
was sent home with his scrip
crammed full with meat, bread,
dressed doves and other birds
for Lamo and Myrtle's table
while the frosted earth stalled.
So Daphnis left, deliberately
embracing Chloe last so that he
could keep her kisses ripe
while his lips went unwiped.
Yet he returned many times
so that with like stratagems
the winter freeze did not rot
the fruit of their love one mote.

Finally the snow was gone
and the land once again green.
Flocks frolicked to the fields

Chloe and Daphnis in the lead
as the kin of shepherd elders.
And immediately they hared
to the Nymphs' cave, to Pan's
statue with his pipe and then
to the oak where they embraced
close to their herds, and kissed.
To embellish the statues
they gathered flowers in bloom
which Zephyrus and the sun
had sparked into life: bunches
of violets, daffodils and more:
primroses from a spring lawn.
Then they toasted the gods
with quick milk from the goats,
and played the pipe to provoke
birds to sing to their music;
some countered from the groves
in jugging and chirruping tones
with tales of Tereus and Itys.
And everywhere with relish
they heard piped sheep bleat,
saw leaping lambs retreat
to suckle under vigilant ewes
and barren sheep pursued
by rams to make them stand.
They saw the jounce and
tilting of male goats – the way,
intent on coupling, they
parried the truckling juveniles
which saw themselves as rivals.

The old herders seeing all this
were hosed down by Venus,
but the young, itching and lewd,
fired up by what they heard
and saw began to chase

for more than a plain embrace.
Daphnis as much as anyone
being now a young swain
ardent after winter's check
kissed with a fury, necked
and nestled with vigour
more venturous than before
and begged Chloe to let him
have his way and lie with him
naked longer than they had
hitherto done, since, he said,
there was nothing left to try
of old Philetas's remedies
to cure their love sickness.
Yet Chloe wondered what else
there could be but to kiss;
how could it possibly heal
a boy to lie with a naked girl?

Could she not see what rams do
to ewes and what billy goats do
to nannies Daphnis asked her;
how they grazed together after
and did not run away, happy
in each other's company.

But did he not also see, she said,
that she-goats and ewes stand
to receive their eager mates,
yet he wanted her prostrate
naked on the ground, whereas
they remained in their fleeces.
So Daphnis was persuaded,
and lying confused by her side
abided there for an age
not knowing how to manage
what he was mad for. Firstly

he positioned her to copy
the goats, but failed feebly.
Then, frustrated, he sat Chloe
up again despairing that
he was far less adroit
in the mysteries and art
of loving than any goat.

But Daphnis had a neighbour
– Chromis, a landowner
though by now an old churl.
He had married a city girl –
young, fair and pretty, one
whose skin was too porcelain
for such a country clown.
Lycenia was her name
and, seeing Daphnis each day
drive his herd to the plains
and home again at dusk, she
slyly schemed for him to be
her lover. So, ever opportune,
she caught him on his own
and gave him a fine new pipe,
rich honeycombs and a scrip
made of the finest stag-hide,
yet dare not speak her mind
knowing he cared for Chloe.
For every rustic could see
they were utterly besotted
by the winks, nodding heads
and petting which betrayed them.

Then one morning she misled
Chromis into thinking that
she had left for the market,
and followed the sweethearts
at a distance instead, darting
into thickets where she hid.

From such cover she overheard
all that they said, could see
all that they did. So it was she
discovered their despair
and saw how to manoeuvre
Daphnis to slake her lust.

The next day, under the ruse
of gossiping with town folk,
she approached the oak
where the lovers sat together,
feigned to be in bother
and begged Daphnis for help.
She had seen an eagle swoop
on her best goose, she said,
but being heavy it failed
to carry it to its eyrie
on a high crag and its prey
has fallen into a far copse
lucky for the giddy goose.
She pleaded with Daphnis
for the sake of the Nymphs
and Pan to rescue her pet
from the wood and garrotte
the bird so it would not swoop
again on lambs and whelps.
Chloe could easily tend
both herds being a friend
of his goats too. So Daphnis,
unsuspecting, took up his
staff and trailed Lycenia
far from Chloe till they came
into the nub of the wood
where she asked if they could
sit for a while by a fountain.
From here her web was spun.

Daphnis, I know you love Chloe.
I learnt this from the Nymphs
last night. The tears you cried
over your love I visualised
in my dream, and I have been
ordered to save you and train
you in love's many ways; not
just kissing and caressing; not
just what you see the rams and
goats do but I am commanded
to coach you in many more
lingering sweeter pleasures
than those. If you wish to rid
your pain and scratch the itch
of that bliss you crave denied
to you so long, let us gratify
the Nymphs. Be my novice
and I will be your mistress.

At this Daphnis, being but a
peasant herder made of clay
and all afire with desire,
could not contain his ardour
but threw himself at her feet
eagerly begging her to teach
him in those arts so that he
could hone them on Chloe;
he would treat his learning
as a rare and wonderful thing
sent from the gods. For her
great kindness he would offer
her a suckling kid, cheeses
from fresh milk as well as
the she-goat it came from.
And so Lycenia, finding him
impatient and sharp-stropped
beyond her remotest hopes,

plunged into her love class.
She bade him sit as close
to her as he possibly could
so that they might kiss and hug
as much as he did with Chloe,
and take her in his arms to lie
together on the ground. She,
finding him primed and greedy,
slipped slickly beneath him
and shepherded his limbs
to where they longed to be.
What followed came naturally,
nothing strange or coarse
and though she wanted more
when it was over, Daphnis
in all his innocence wished
to break away urgently
and try this lesson on Chloe,
show her all he had learned
afraid that if he remained
he may forget a trick or two.
But Lycenia said no.

Remember this, Daphnis:
I am a mature woman; this
skill of mine is well practised;
another taught me this bliss
and had my maidenhead
for his pains. On the other hand
if you do the same with Chloe
she may scream, cry and bleed
as if she were wounded. But
have no barter with that.
Once you have won her over
bring her here; if she roars
and screeches no one will heed
her and if indeed she bleeds,

there's a fountain close by.
But never forget – it was I,
not her, who made a man of you.

With that she kissed him anew
and flounced to another limb
of the wood as if to comb
it for her bogus goose,
leaving Daphnis to muse
on her words which quickly
melted in his fire for Chloe.
For he dare not press her
beyond her displeasure
and would have to cease
his kissing and caresses
if she screamed as against a foe,
or poured forth tears of sorrow,
never mind bleed to death.
For he still recalled the depth
of the beating he sustained
from the Methymnians,
and therefore feared blood
having no notion that it could
flow from other than a wound.
And so he resolved only to woo
and leave the rest to fantasy.

Once free of the forest trees
he came across Chloe seated
plaiting a garland of violets,
and told her the fake tale
of the goose and the eagle.
Then he held her and kissed
her as he had rehearsed
with his tutor Lycenia since
there was no peril in a kiss.
Chloe levelled his chaplet

and pecked his blond tresses
loving them more than violets.
Next she passed him the best
simnel cake from her scrip
then snatched it from his lips
with the speed of a pecking bird
after loose seed on the earth.

Eating in between each kiss
they saw a fishing boat pass.
All was calm. The sea asleep
so that its oars must sweep
the still water at speed, for
they were rushing in their haul
freshly salted for the plates
of Mitylene's good and great.
They sang, as all seamen sing
to drown the tedium of rowing
and among them a rare voice
led the chorus – Celeustes
was his name and his shanties
rose to the crew's rich cadence
as they harmonised to sing
the refrain. The open sea
swallowed their singing; yet,
rowing tightly by the jut
of a vast scut promontory
in the horns of a cloistered bay,
their chorus to the words
of Celeustes was heard
far inland where the valleys
received it like conch shells,
and to the clatter of their oars
freely returned their barcarolle.

Firstly came a sea serenade,
its echo heard in the fields;

yet it was the crew singing
from the pinnace lingering
on the waves which absorbed
Daphnis; and while the boat
slid by like a sleek swan he
committed the tunes to memory
so that he could replay
them on his pipe. But Chloe
heard echoes for the first time
and looked out to sea to find
where Celeustes sang; then to
the woods for the singers who
answered his song. And when
they passed there was silence
in the valley and she asked
if there was another sea masked
by the headland with yet
a second boat in full throat
singing the same sea tunes
although silent now too.

Daphnis kissed her innocence,
placed his chaplet on her head
and began the tale of Echo
wheedling from her first an oath
to give him ten more kisses
as his reward at its finish:

There are many kinds of Nymphs:
the Meliae, the Dryads, the Eliis
– all beautiful and musical. Echo
was the daughter of one though
mortal since her father was
human, but also beauteous
for her mother was ravishing.
She was schooled by the Nymphs
and taught by the Muses to sing,

play the pipe, lyre and lute; in
short every musical instrument
so that as an adolescent
in the full flush of chastity
she danced for the Nymphs
and sang with the Muses in key.
But she shunned male company,
both men and gods, because
she cherished being virtuous.
This pleased Pan not one bit
since she would not permit
him to approach. So, angry,
he spread lust among the
herders, and like rabid dogs
they set about her and chopped
her to bits casting her limbs
in the dirt. Yet she sang still
and obeying the Nymphs
the good Earth took her in
and Echo's severed limbs
purled beneath the ground and
imitated god, beast and man
– even Pan, who began to
search the plains, not to
seduce her, but to see
who played as good as he.

The tale told, Chloe gave him
leave for a landslide of kisses.

Spring's story too was soon told
as Summer's myths unfolded
in the sun's wandering fervour.
Daphnis swam in swarming rivers,
played his pipe to the pines while
Chloe bathed in the kind smiles
of springs, her sweet voice vying

with nightingales. Some mornings
they hunted the prattling cicada
or grasshopper; on other days
they picked flowers, shook trees
for their fruit or lay at their ease
together on the goatskin
they took everywhere with them.
And Chloe would have certainly
lost her maidenhead had he
been undaunted by the thought
of blood. Therefore, distraught
that love would defy reason
he asked her to lie with him
scantily dressed less and less
making Chloe curious,
though because she was shy
she never asked him why.

That summer she had numerous
suitors from the length of Lesbos
bringing gifts and promises
of a handsome dowry to Dryas.
This excited Nape and she
began to impress on Chloe
that at her age it was the norm
to no longer live at home
since it may happen one day
she would lose her virginity
for an apple or a wild rose
and land some recreant rogue
as husband. It was for the best
that she should be mistress
in her own home, take a groom
and permit them more room.

But Dryas was in two minds:
preferring not to decline

these many lavish gifts for his
peasant daughter shepherdess.
Yet at other times he thought
she merited more than rewards
offered by some lumpkin.
Moreover, if she ever alighted
on her true father she might
make Dryas and all his kin
rich and happy. So he bid
her beaux have patience while
he endured their venal will.
When Chloe learned of this
she screened her new sadness
not wanting Daphnis hurt.
Yet when he pressed her
without response he became
more vexed than had he known.
So she gave in and disclosed
how Nape had incited Dryas
to marry her off, and he
had not refused but had only
deferred it until the harvest.
At this Daphnis was crest-
fallen and in despair. He
sat down and wept bitterly
saying that if she went away
he and her sheep would die
pining for their shepherdess.
Then he grew more audacious
and resolved to turn Dryas
by being one of the wooers;
a plan to become favoured
above the tups of the herd.

But one thing irked him over
all else – that his father Lamo
was not rich, though to be one

of the suitors was certain
to be the best furrow to sow.
And, fearing to beard Lamo,
he spoke first to Myrtle telling
her not only of his feelings
but his wish to marry Chloe;
in bed later she told Lamo.
Yet Lamo checked her grimly
angry at her sudden whim
to match a shepherd's offspring
with their boy whose trappings
hinted at a huge fortune;
he told her, if ever his true
parents be found, they would
not only free them for good
but grant them a great acreage.
But she knew love's scourge
and, in case Daphnis despaired
and took his own life, tailored
this response to her sad son.

Thanks to our lack of fortune
it would be best if you sought
a wealthy wife. For certain sure
Dryas will look for a rich suitor.
But tell Chloe to prod her father
not to ask for much in gifts,
then you may not seem so bereft.
For I'm convinced she loves you
and would rather be true
a thousand times to a needy
Adonis than a rich monkey.

But Myrtle was certain that
Dryas would give no clout
to the marriage as there were
already many wealthy wooers,

and Daphnis would be prised
from his broken heart's desire
just like a lych-gate beggar.
So fearing possible failure
Daphnis once again implored
the Nymphs for their support.
The eldest entered his sleep;
dreaming he heard her speak:

Daphnis, you will have riches
enough to win the will of Dryas.
The Methymnian boat which,
because goats ate its bindings
was carried out to sea by
offshore winds, was eventually
dashed in a wild tempest
on the rocks and all perished
who served in her. Yet the tide
washed up a purse and inside
were three thousand drachmas.
You'll find it covered in ooze
close to a dead dolphin which
the curious will never approach
because of its repellent stench.
Quick, hurry! Take it hell-bent
to Dryas and be poor no more.

Day dawned and Daphnis tore
from his bed with all the joy
that a heart could hold. The boy
hurried his goats to the fields
and, kissing Chloe quick, fled
to the beach as if for a swim,
though to look for the dolphin
and drachmas spent by the sea.
Soon the stench found him. He
eased off the kelp and under-

neath was a purse full of silver;
into his scrip it went as he
praised the Nymphs and the sea.
Though he worked in the fields
he now felt closer to the tides
because they made his marriage
possible. And so, feeling rich,
more than any other man
who lived in the region,
he fled to find his Chloe
to tell her of the dream, show
her the purse and ask her to mind
the flocks until he returned.
Then, with a strut as grandiose
as any lord, he burst in on Dryas
finding him with Nape at work
on the threshing floor and broke
boldly about marrying Chloe
appealing for her liberty:

For I can play the panpipe
well, harvest and plant vines,
know when and how to plough,
and whip the wind to winnow
corn. As for my expertise
with herds Chloe is my witness.
Fifty she-goats I had from my
father Lamo and have nigh
doubled that number. Also
I have reared hardy stud-goats,
whereas before we needed
other men's beasts to breed.
Am I not a swain known
to you, one who will in no
way shirk his work? I had
a goat for my nurse just as
Chloe had a ewe. In all this

I best the other suitors, riches
I have too. They may give you
the scrag-end of a few
sheep or goats, a rascally
pair of oxen with barely
enough corn for your hens.
But from me, look within –
three thousand drachmas!
Only, don't tell anyone else
not least my father Lamo.

This said he handed it over to
Nape and Dryas, embracing them;
and when they saw the vivid trim
of so much sudden money
they promptly promised Chloe
agreeing to press for Lamo's yes.
Nape remained with Daphnis
driving oxen over the floor
to trample the ears of corn,
chaffing the grain with a hurdle
of sharp-honed stones while
Dryas hid the drachma hoard
with Chloe's rich infant clothes
and hurried to Lamo's home
to plead for the bridegroom.
He found them grim and gloomy
bagging newly winnowed barley
– theirs had been a poor harvest.
Dryas consoled them as best
he could, saying it was in every
place the same sorry story.

He asked for Lamo's blessing
on their children's wedding
telling him that though others
had made generous offers

he would accept nothing
but rather give something.
For Daphnis and Chloe had
grown up together, he said,
to lead their flocks as one,
had nursed a love so strong
it would be hard to destroy
so they may as well marry;
and he added much more made
heady by so many drachmas.

So Lamo dwelt on Daphnis's
neediness no more since Dryas
did not slight his simple status,
nor the bleakness of his house,
but worried instead that Daphnis
might yet be a noble prince:

Indeed, you do well to prefer
your neighbour to strangers,
not prizing riches more than
proud poverty. May Pan
and the Nymphs bless you
for that, Dryas. As for me I do
not stand in the way of this
union. It would make sense,
being old and in need
of help in my daily grind,
to be allied to your kin.
How I wish for that! In
addition Chloe is a pearl,
a true and beautiful girl
desired by not a few. Yet,
as you know, since I am helot
my lord must be petitioned
and asked for his sanction.
So let us therefore postpone

the nuptials until the autumn
when, I am told, he'll return
again from the city. Then
shall they be married. Yet
meanwhile they must love
as siblings. Moreover, chew
on this, Dryas: the boy you
are in earnest over may be
far better than you and me.

And Lamo embraced Dryas
inviting him to sit and carouse
while the midday sun was high
before civilly seeing him away.
Yet Dryas had not understood
Lamo's curious parting words
and felt compelled to query
who Daphnis could possibly be:

Daphnis was certainly reared
by a goat as though the gods
had willed it, and is noble-fair
unlike his flat-nosed father
and his frowzy dowdy spouse.
And who would have supposed
a lowly goatherd would have
so many drachmas in his bag?
Had Daphnis also been exposed
like Chloe at birth? Did Lamo
have luck too, finding a baby? And
with the infant did he also find
such highborn goods as Chloe's.
O Mighty Pan! Beloved Nymphs!
If he has found his own parents
Chloe's may also soon be met.

Such brooding ideas churned
in his mind before he returned

to find a breathless Daphnis
waiting for Lamo's response;
and, hailing him as his new son,
he promised they would soon
be married. He gave Daphnis
his right hand and swore Chloe
would be no man's wife but his.
And so without dining Daphnis
flew to her quicker than thought
and full of rejoicing brought
her his nuptial news and more,
kissing not furtively as before
but as his wife, helping her
to carry the milk pales, eager
to mould her cheeses and feed
her lambs with his kids. These
chores done they washed for
supper, feasted then looked for
fruit – plump pears and apples:
the windfalls smelt ambrosial
with the fragrance of wine
and those unpicked and high
glowed like liquid gold.

One orchard tree stood alone
with no leaves and no fruit
but for one single apple left
unpicked as high as a spire:
a red russet in royal attire
radiant with a rich aroma
too near the sky to gather,
waiting for a swain in love.
Reckless Daphnis resolved
on it and would not heed
Chloe's forbidding pleas.
Displeased she strutted off
forsaking him for her flock.

But Daphnis climbed anyway
and plucked the fruit for Chloe;
then followed her to the fields
but seeing her angry pleaded:

Many sun-kissed hours reared
this apple born of an honest tree,
ripened in sun-glow, preserved
by luck and care. I could never
leave it once seen by your eyes
in case it fell from on high
and a grazing cow crushed it,
or following the maggot's bite
time rotted it in the field.
For the victor of her beauty
Venus gave no other prize,
and I award it you as witness
to your matching loveliness.
Remember, Paris was a base
shepherd as I am a goatherd
in these blissful Methylene fields.

With that he gave her the fruit
and she hugged and rooted
him with love so that Daphnis
in no way regretted his rashness,
for one kiss was more valuable
to him than any Golden Apple.

Fourth Canto

Summer had heeled to Autumn
when Lamo's servant came
with news from Mitylene
that their lord would return
at harvest time to examine
what mischief the invasion
of the Methymnians had done
to his domain. Poor Lamo spun
in his panic to prepare
for his master's pleasure.
He flushed the fountains
so that the water was clean,
and scoured his cottage lest
animal stench offended.
He groomed the garden with
strenuous pluck and pull till
fragrant again it flourished fair.
His grove would do honour
to royalty since it crowned
four acres of high ground
with ferocious fecundity
strutting every species of tree:
pomegranate, pear and apple,
orange, fig, olive and myrtle.
Rare vines with luscious grapes
fraternised with plums and dates.
Much burgeoned there, sown
or grafted, not least the pines,
cypresses, laurels and planes
which ivy wantonly entwined,
while unbrided produce dared
to marry with ripening grapes.

As though within a fort
low-bearing trees bore fruit
mobbing with their opulence
yet more o'erbrimming berries.
And further out woodland trees
flaunted the ferocious face
of an impregnable stockade
bearded with a balustrade
of low sentinel hedges. Lanes
and glades defined the garden
and arcing boughs atop greeted
each other's limbs and leaves.
You would not think of Nature
but one man's architecture.
Neither did the beds and banks
lack colour from their plants,
with roses, hyacinths and lilies
set by hand among pimpernels,
daffodils, violets growing wild.
Spring brought generous shade,
summer symmetry and scent
and autumn the grape harvest;
every season had its fruit.
And from the slopes swooped
down an imposing outlook
to the valley fields where flocks
of contented cattle nibbled.
Beyond, the bright sea, stippled
with sailing boats and pinnaces,
added to the spell and grace
of this idyllic demi-paradise.

There, posturing in classic style,
stood the temple of Dionysus,
its guardian, the altar discussed
and flattered by simpering ivy

with vine boughs snaking by.
In the shrine's interior
frescoes plashed the drama
of Dionysus and his story:
Semele giving birth, Ariadne
asleep, Lycurgus bound in
chains, pitiful Pentheus torn
limb from limb, the Indians
defeated, the Tyrrhenian
sailors enchanted, Satyrs
and Bacchantes everywhere.
Neither was Pan neglected
in this place of perfect aspect
for, piping high from a crag,
he was seen striking up a jig
for peasant women to dance
and stomp in the wine press.

So, in this god-given garden
Lamo slaved tired and bent
cutting and pruning the dry
withered heads to inspire
his vines to increased growth.
He crowned Dionysus with
lush wreaths and chased water
from the fountains to pour
into the beds and borders.
Other parts he watered
from a spa Daphnis had found
and named after himself; and
set the young herder to fatten
his flock for ducal inspection.

But Daphnis went untroubled:
he had already doubled
his flock having lost none
to wolves; his goats had grown

fatter than all the other sheep;
and since he had a great need
for his master to approve
his marriage he grew obsessive,
driving out his flock at dawn
and herding them home again
late evening. Twice a day
he watered them, let them graze
the best pasture and was careful
to clean his milking vessels,
keeping a full stock of pales,
piggins, presses and crates.
He was negligent in nothing,
shining goat horns with resin
and combing their fleeces
to slicken them like sheet ice –
anyone would have believed
his was Pan's very own herd.
Chloe too helped with the goats
and Daphnis thought it most
to do with her hand and eye
that his flock looked so spry.

Then, while both were busy
a messenger came from the city
with orders that the grapes
be gathered in with all haste;
that he would remain while
the must was made, then retire
to the city to fetch his lord
once the harvest was stored.
His name was Eudromus,
and he watched their merriness
with pleasure as the harvest
was garnered: the grapes wrested
from vines and portered to
the presses, the must produced

and tipped into tuns. Yet some
of the busiest bunches
they left high on the branch
to show folk what an avalanche
of fruit the harvest had provoked.
And when the moment knocked
at last for Eudromus to go away
Daphnis gave him a fine array
of simple gifts: splendid
pressed cheeses, a young kid
and a shaggy white fleece
to warm him as he raced
around to deliver dispatches.
Eudromus was bewitched;
he embraced Daphnis saying
he would be commending
him to his lord; then vanished.

However, before long Daphnis
buckled under leaden thought,
and Chloe was also distraught
that he, still callow and green
fresh from his goats and sheep,
must in no small way endure
the potent presence of his lord,
of whom he knew nothing but
his name. Moreover she tutted
over his likely behaviour
in front of their many betters
being but a swain, and agonised
that their marriage might
wither like a deciduous leaf.
Kissing seemed their only relief
but as they embraced as close
as strung beads there was no
respite from fear, and their love
became pinching and pensive.

Yet, they were soon distracted.
Lampis, a depraved, abject
herder, was one of the suitors
who had done Dryas favours
and given him gifts. He knew
if their lord did not refuse
to allow the marriage it would
proceed. He therefore construed
a cunning ruse to beguile
and disaffect their master. Alive
to the pleasure he relished in
Lamo's garden he fixed
to plunder it and ruin
his reputation. Afraid to down
Lamo's trees for fear of the din
he resolved to terrorise
his flower beds, and at night
hacked through hedges to root
out countless plants; he tore
up some by the stem, like a boar
trampled others and then fled
into the darkness undetected.

Morning brought Lamo's saunter
into the garden to water
his flowers; but when he saw
the desolation there he clawed
at his clothes and railed
to the gods so loud that Myrtle
left what she was doing, ran
with Daphnis to him and
they all cursed and cried
fearing what their lord might
say. Any passing stranger
would have wept too for
little was left of the garden's

beauty; all was mud and ruin.
What blooms survived feigned
their natural allure; flattened,
they failed to appease the bees
busy about their grisly elegy
while embattled Lamo raved:

My poor rose beds raided
and wrecked! And the violets,
torn, trounced and violated!
What demon dared demolish
my daffodils and hyacinths!
Spring may as well be sterile,
the summer sun will smile
on none of these and at autumn
there can be no bobbing shrubs,
no sorrel leaves for garlands.
Dionysus, god of the garden,
whom I have often crowned
with the blooms you quickened
with your breath, did you
not pity their agony? How may
I show this garden to my lord!
How he will gnash his words
and curse! He will hang me
for a rogue from a pine tree
like Marsyas! And maybe
Daphnis too if he believes
his goats are to blame!

His tears scalded his face
with sorrow for his fallen flowers
while Chloe cried for her lover
praying that their lord might
not come. She passed the night
in misery imagining Daphnis
taken, tortured and whipped.

But when Eudromus returned
he brought word that their lord
planned to visit in three days,
but that his only son, Astylus,
would come on the morrow. So
they took Eudromus deep into
their brittle confidence to see
what might be done, for he
had taken a shine to Daphnis.
And he advised them to enlist
Astylus' help since he claimed
no little influence over him
(they being almost brothers)
and this plan held them together.

At dawn Astylus arrived
with his man Gnatho riding
on horseback; the lord's heir
had little use for a razor
but Gnatho's beard was stiff.
Lamo, Myrtle and Daphnis
flung themselves at his feet,
and most meekly entreated
mercy for a luckless man
who had wronged no one,
to spare him his father's fury.
They swiftly explained how he
had borne a huge misfortune
but Astylus, seeing the garden,
made light of Lamo's ruin
and vowed to seek a pardon
by blaming horses nearby
which may have likely shied,
broken their bridles and
like a tidal wave flattened
his flower beds and plants.
Relieved at this lenience

Lamo and Myrtle beseeched
the gods to grant him riches.
They gave him young kids,
cream cheeses, hens and chicks,
bunches of grapes on the vine,
apples on the bough and wine
from the best tuns on Lesbos.
Astylus coddled their kindness,
then went hunting, for he was
sportive and given over to chase
his pleasure in the countryside.

But Gnatho, a coarse man, liked
to quaff and carouse until drunk;
his pleasure stocked his great gut.
He had eyed Daphnis lewdly
rating him the rarest beauty
of all the youths in Mitylene,
and deviously determined
to seduce him, imagining
it would be no difficult thing
he being a simple goatherd.
So when Astylus rode
away to hunt, Gnatho sped
to the pastures where he met
Daphnis, ostensibly to see
his rarest goats but in reality
to lust after their herder.
With one arm on his shoulder
he flattered Daphnis's hair,
asked him to play a pastoral air
and vowed to seek his freedom
having some jurisdiction
and sway over his great lord,
so wooing him with easy words.
And as light failed in the evening
and Daphnis set upon driving

his herd home Gnatho picked
his time, ran after him at a lick
and, kissing his new friend
over and over, sidled behind
him in an inept attempt to do
what a ram does to a ewe.
But Daphnis resisting cried:

That all male animals ride
females is only natural
but a ram mounting his equal
is not right! Nor do cock birds
mate cocks! You are absurd!

Then Gnatho grappled with him
to have his way but Daphnis
was too strong and fought off
the pot-valiant besotted sot
who was barely able to stand,
knocked him to the ground
and fled leaving him dazed.
From then on Daphnis grazed
his herd where he could be
near Chloe, and Gnatho teased
him no more finding Daphnis
still desirous but too doughty.

Soon Dionysophanes,
their lord, arrived with his
consort, Clearista, attended
by chariots, carriages, footmen,
maidservants and slaves.
This noble Dionysophanes
was tall-erect but turning grey,
yet still able to wrestle and slay
younger men in the games.
He was rich and acclaimed

honest, cultured, fair but firm,
and on his arrival he performed
a sacrifice to the agrarian
gods: Demeter, Dionysus, Pan
and the Nymphs, and presented
a vat of wine to the peasants.
Then he asked to survey
his domain to see how the clay
had ploughed, how the grapes
grew generously, what shape
the vineyards were in, how
Lamo's garden looked now
having been informed of its
ruin by no less than Astylus
himself. And indeed overall
he was pleased and grateful,
honouring the relieved Lamo
by granting him his freedom.

Later he visited the fields
to see the goats and herds
while Chloe fled to the trees
shy of such exalted company.
But Daphnis stood resolute
with his shag fleece about
his shoulders and a new bag,
fresh cheeses in one hand
while leading a suckling kid.
If ever Apollo was bid to
serve Laomedon as herdsman
Daphnis was his simulacrum.
Blushing without one word
eyes aground, he gave the lord
these gifts as Lamo spoke.

This is the keeper of the goats
you gave me, Sire, and look!

He has doubled the flock!
See how plump they are now,
how thick their fleeces are, how
strong their horns. They know
music too and do whatever
he commands when he plays.

Clearista, hearing him say
this and wanting to see proof,
asked him to pipe a tune
promising Daphnis a chiton,
mantle and new shoes. So when
they were seated comfortably
he stood under a beech tree
and applied the pipe to his lips.
First be blew at a low pitch
and at once the goats rose
their ears pricked at the noise.
Then he played a pastoral trill
and the goats grazed again till
sweeter notes bade them lie
serene and rest. By and by
he struck a more urgent tone
warning of the wolf, and as one
his flock fled to the far wood.
After a while he piped a loud
recall and they quickly thawed
from the trees and poured
round his feet – never did a lord
have such obsequious accord
from his maids and servants.

The crowd cheered such talent,
none more so that Clearista;
moved by his pipe's charisma
she presented him his rewards.
Then they all turned homewards

to feast, but sent back the pick
of the banquet which Daphnis
shared in the fields with Chloe.
They relished many delicacies,
confections and city desserts
while hoping they had deserved
their lord's treasured favour
so that they may live together.

But Gnatho was more fired up
than ever and empty was his cup
unless he had his Daphnis.
So, catching Astylus at his ease
in the garden he drew him near
to the temple of Dionysus where
he knelt and slickly entreated
him kissing his hands and feet:

Master, I am done for!
I, who loved nothing better
than a laden table and swore
there was nothing more
desirable than good wine.
I, who always fondly dined
on your desserts sweeter than
the fairest boys in Mitylene.
I, who know that nothing is
tastier than sweet Daphnis,
may as well cease feasting
on the freshest meat and fish.
Nothing would please me more
than to be a goat to be near
Daphnis, eat grass and leaves
at his feet, hear his pipe, feed
off the fruit from his grove.
Save Gnatho, defend my love!
Else I will take this dagger

and stab myself before his door,
and you will never know
me more, poor devoted Gnatho.

Astylus, of unstinting spirit
and as one yet to be lit
by love's tormenting fire,
could not suffer him to cry
kissing his feet over and over;
so he promised to ask his father
for Daphnis to be his servant
in Mitylene, thus convenient
for being at Gnatho's beck.
Yet, with a smile of regret
he asked whether Gnatho
did not feel debased to be so
enamoured of Lamo's son,
wanting to lie with a swain
who kept goats, seeing as
their odour was so obnoxious.
Gnatho answered with a wit
honed in city streets and inns.

Epicures do not worry over
such frothy affairs. Wherever
we brush against beauty we fall
under its spell. Some will
love a tree, some a cataract,
some a beast. And what man
would not pity the miserable
lover who is fatally shackled
to what he fears to love?
But I, loving a servant, will live
within the pale of innocence.
Do you not see that his tresses
fall like hyacinths! His eyes
are like gems of glistering topaz

in gilt settings! How deeply
flushed are his virgin cheeks,
how roseate his lips, his teeth
are like pearls! Who could keep
from kissing his face? And if
I love a herder then I merely
imitate the gods, for Anchises
was a herdsman, yet was prized
by Aphrodite; Branchius
was a goatherd possessed
by Apollo, and Ganymede was
a shepherd and yet great Zeus
desired him. Therefore in truth
you should not scorn this youth
because he keeps a flock, for do
not his own goats love him too?

Astylus smiled observing how
love turns clods into Platos.
He resolved to speak to his
father about poor Daphnis.
But Eudromus had overheard
and was bitterly disturbed
that such a flower of beauty
should ever be plucked by
so foul a fellow. And so
he told Daphnis and Lamo
what had been said and Daphnis
was cut to the quick and fixed
to either run away with Chloe
or dispatch them both to the
Elysian Fields. Then Lamo led
Myrtle out of doors and said:

What shall we do? We are
done for! Is now the hour
to come clean and testify

how a baby was left to die
in a bleak place, and worse
how a goat became his nurse?
For, by the great god Pan
and all the Nymphs, even
though I may well be gaoled
like an ox locked in his stall,
I'll no longer quell my voice
but tell how I came across
the abandoned infant, how
he was nursed and then show
the chattels found with him.
Then Gnatho, that ruffian,
may know who he dares to love.
Go, bring me the infant goods!

Meanwhile Astylus wrested
his lord from sleep to request
that Daphnis be released
from his herd and commence
his service in Mitylene;
he said he was a steady-keen
and one Gnatho would favour
with city ways. His father
readily agreed and sent for
Lamo without further thought.
He told Lamo that Daphnis
must now attend on Astylus
in the city and no longer be
a keeper of goats and he
gifted him two herdsmen
in recompense. And when
Lamo saw Astylus's men hug
each other for joy because
they were to have more help
he knew he must speak up:

Sire. Please heed this true tale
I, an old man, am about to tell.
I swear by the Nymphs and Pan
that I will not lie one smidgen.
I am not the father of Daphnis!
And Myrtle is not one bit
the mother to so faithful
and dear a boy. His natural
parents abandoned him but
I found him suckled by a goat
where he had been exposed.
When the goat died I hollowed
a grave for it in appreciation
beyond the edge of the garden
because it had mothered him.
Yet some personal things
I found by him hinted at
great wealth and exalted rank.
I have always kept them close.
To serve your son, Astylus,
is one thing but I can't agree
to Daphnis being abused freely
by this drunken dog, Gnatho;
to be the slave to such a rogue
who'd demean him in Mitylene
as his lover, his Ganymede.

Lamo ended his plea in tears
and Gnatho raved, grew fierce
and made to use his cudgel but
Dionysophanes, disturbed
by what he heard, silenced
him with a glower and at once
sternly demanded to know
the untainted truth from Lamo
with no overripe lies sown
in a row to keep him at home.

And Lamo stood by that he said
swearing by the gods he would
submit to any torture if he lied.
So the lord drew his lady aside
to weigh all the possible reasons
Lamo might have to lie when
promised two new herdsmen.
How could such a simple peon
plan such a story? Besides,
it seemed absurd that his wife,
that gnarled old oak, could
bear such a beautiful bud!
So he proposed to examine
the possessions to determine
whether they did indeed reach
out to a noble heritage.

Myrtle fetched all that had
been kept years in an old bag;
and Lord Dionysophanes,
astonished, cried out to Zeus
when he drew out the mantle
of purple, the golden buckle
and dagger with its ivory stock.
He called in his wife to look,
and when she recognised them
calling on the Fates she exclaimed:

Are not these the very effects
left with our son at our behest,
exposed in the open fields by
Sophrosyne? This is our child!
Daphnis without question,
the goat herder, is our son!

And as she rejoiced her lord
caressed and kissed the hoard
crying over it in great joy;

and Astylus, hearing of his boy
brother as in a cloudburst
shed his cape to be the first
to run to him with a kiss.
But Daphnis, seeing Astylus
with others rush him in a squall
and hearing his name called
over and over, thought they
were coming to take him away.
He ditched his pipe and scrip
and ran off in fright to fling
himself over the nearest cliff;
and would have done so if
Astylus had not checked his
rashness by shouting thus:

Daphnis, don't be afraid!
I'm your brother and they
who were your lord and lady
are your parents. This day
Lamo has told us everything
about the goat and rich things
abandoned with you. Please!
Turn! See! I rejoice in the news.
Quick, embrace me. Do not die.
By the Nymphs I do not lie.

Calmed by his words he waited
for Astylus to come and fate
blessed them as they hugged.
Soon the others caught up –
his new noble parents,
their housemaids and servants.
They anointed their happiness
with tears of joy but it was
his father and mother Daphnis
clung to more than most as if

he had known them forever
and would never be severed.
At the village they dressed
him befitting his new status
and he stood at his father's side
who spoke to the curious crowd:

My Sons, I married when
I was very young and soon
became a happy father –
first a son, then a daughter,
later Astylus came. Certain
that we had enough children
we exposed the next child,
a boy, to the elements to lie
with his chattels around him.
But the Fates have their schemes:
my eldest children passed away
of fever both on the same day.
Yet you, Daphnis, were saved
to cheer us in our old age.
However, do not take it ill
by thinking us cruel or evil
that we relinquished you,
though it was a sad thing to do.
And you, Astylus, must not resent
Daphnis's new inheritance.
For any wise man will tell you
there's nothing of more value
than to have a loyal brother.
Therefore, love each other
and liken yourselves to kings
for I'll leave you large holdings,
loyal hardworking menials,
gold and silver, and all
that privilege highly rates,
excepting for this estate

which I give to Daphnis alone
plus Myrtle and Lamo's goats.

Yet almost before he had done
Daphnis looked about him:

Father, you've reminded me!
By now the goats will be thirsty
and expect to be led to water
while I loll and idle here.

At this they all laughed since,
though now ennobled, Daphnis
still thought himself a goatherd;
but another went in his stead.
Afterwards they sacrificed
to Zeus, caroused and feasted.
Only Gnatho was absent
since in a spineless sweat
he took refuge in the temple
of Dionysus to shamble
through the ashes of the night.

Before long the news was out:
their liege had found his son!
Daphnis the herder had become
the master of their estate.
Peasants came early and late
from miles around to applaud
and bring tributes to their lord,
Chloe's father being the first.
And he granted them a feast
to celebrate his son's return
with huge urns of spicy wine
and breads of the finest flour,
exotic flavours of water-fowl,
suckling pigs, dainty pastries,

sweet wafers, simnels and pies
while sacrifices floated aloft
votives to the island's gods.

Daphnis set to gathering
all his former belongings
to kindle on the altar.
To Dionysus he offered
his scrip and fleece mantle;
to Pan his pipe and whistle,
his crook and wooden pails
to the Nymphs. Yet because
they had served him well,
almost a part of him, he wept
over each valediction and did
not offer up the pails until
he had used them once more;
nor his mantle till he had worn
it on his back one more time;
and certainly not his pipe
before he had played a tune
or two again. How he rued
each oblation, stroked them,
called each goat by its name.
Then he went to the fountain
where he had been many times
with Chloe for one last sip
of its pearls before he slipped
away leaving his love alone
in misery to weep and groan!

Daphnis has forgotten me
immersed in his new prosperity.
Why did I make him swear
also on his goat's life. Were
the oaths we made in the cave
not enough for the Nymphs?

Clearly he has forgotten them!
And when he sacrificed to Pan
and the Nymphs, he did not
even look around for me. What
if he has found another instead
among his new mother's maids?
But I wish him well. Life ceases.
I cannot live without my Daphnis.

Daphnis thus distracted, Lampis
the herder went after Chloe
with his men to seize the girl
thinking Daphnis, now a noble,
would no longer want her.
Yet someone heard the uproar,
ran to Nape who told Dryas
and he sped after Daphnis
who listened to him speechless
out of his wits; yet he dare
not involve his father, nor
could he bear to do nothing
so he withdrew into a wing
of the garden in desperation:

Oh, what fateful ill-fortune!
I should be with my flock!
I was happy when I worked
as a herder for then I'd see
Chloe. Now she's been seized
by Lampis, will be with him
tonight while I drown here
in wine and idle pleasure.
I swore by my goat in vain,
and the Nymphs and by Pan!

Yet, skulking in the garden
Gnatho heard his groans

and saw his chance to atone.
He dragooned Astylus' men
asking Dryas to show them
where Lampis lived; then,
at the exact moment when
Chloe was being dragged in,
they rescued her from ruin
and set about his clod clowns.
Gnatho struggled to pinion
Lampis to parade him like
a prisoner, but he was sly
and slunk away a coward.
Then Gnatho, while his lord
slept, returned to find Daphnis
waiting and weeping hapless
in the garden. He placed
Chloe's rescued hand in his,
told him of his intervention
and urged them both to shun
him no more but let him serve
Daphnis lest he would starve.
Daphnis, ecstatic at seeing
Chloe again, was so pleased
he took Gnatho into his service
while begging forgiveness
from Chloe for his neglect.

Nevertheless, with respect
to their betrothal they agreed
to stay silent for now and keep
it secret, telling only Myrtle.
But Dryas thought the full
truth should be told to Lamo
too and undertook to do so.
Then, next morning with her
birth belongings in a coffer
he went to the garden where

their lord was taking the air
with Astylus and Daphnis, and
when all were silent began:

As Lamo spoke out about
events long hidden, so now
must I also. Chloe was never
mine. I did not sire her.
Others were her parents and
a sheep her nurse. I found
her lying in the Nymphaeum.
It was a strange phenomenon
but I brought her home.
Her highborn beauty confirms
she could not ever be ours,
as do the rich things I found
with her, finer than any
shepherd would own. Look! See!
And pray use them to find her
kin so that you may consider
her worthy of marrying Daphnis.

Pausing, Dionysophanes
received his candour well
and seeing Daphnis pallor
he saw love in the boy's tears.
Then, with his son's welfare
uppermost he probed more
deeply; and when he saw her
birth possessions – the mitre,
her rich mantle of gold, her
shoes and personal things –
he summoned Chloe, ordering
her to be merry and glad
because she would soon be wed.
Then Clearista took charge,
dressed her lavishly in such

finery as befitted her son's wife
while Dionysophanes guided
Daphnis to one side to ask him
whether Chloe was a virgin.
And hearing that nothing had
quickened them but chit-chat,
kissing, hugging and oaths,
he was delighted and proposed
a sumptuous banquet so that
her chastity would be fêted
along with her beauty. Dressed
by Clearista in her finest,
her hair festooned and scented
she outshone all the rest
so that even Daphnis found
he scarcely knew her. And,
learning the story of how
she was re-discovered, now
no one believed that Dryas
was her real father, even as
he sat with Lamo, Myrtle,
and Nape at their own table.

More sacrifices were made
on which Chloe consecrated
her old fleece, her scrip,
trinkets, milking pails and pipe.
Then she poured blushing wine
into the grotto fountain
because she had been nursed
there and many times washed
herself in its crystal spray.
She laid garlands on the grave
of her nurse, shown to her by
Dryas, and played her pan pipe
to her own flock. After that
she prayed to the Nymphs that

the parents who forsook her
and exposed her to the air
would not shame her wedding.

Then, with the the feast ending,
Dionysophanes agreed to return
to Mitylene to find Chloe's kin;
and the next morning before
leaving he gave Dryas more
drachmas – yet three thousand;
and an amazed Lamo more land
to graze and sow, plus goats
and goatherds, four stout yoke
of oxen, some winter clothes
and freedom for them both.
Then, with a great ostentation
of horses and covered wagons
the lord left for Mitylene
not arriving until the evening
so no one was about to cheer.
But next morning at their door
a huge throng flocked. Men
and women hurrahed the return
of their lord's boy, even more
when they saw his natural allure.
And the women were pleased
that Clearista had not only
a new son but his bride to boot.
Indeed, their eyes were rooted
by Chloe's glowing beauty
beyond compare. The city
in truth was moved by the
young pair and repeatedly
hailed the coming marriage,
praying it would soon emerge
that her birth was as highborn
as she was fair; indeed certain

of the richer ladies prayed
that they might one day
be mother to such a lass.

Meanwhile Dionysophanes,
burdened with all this mayhem,
fell asleep and had a dream
in which he heard the Nymphs
petition Eros to agree
to the nuptials. He in turn,
his bow and quiver spurned,
commanded him to convene
all the patricians of Mitylene
to a feast and then, with glasses
brimming, to show Chloe's
birth possessions to everyone
as they sang hymns to Hymen.

And so, on waking up he
ordered a great banquet to be
prepared with every delicacy
from the land, marshes, sea
and rivers; and for his guests
he invited the good and great.
Then, when the last great ewer
was filled with wine in honour
of Hermes, Chloe's effects
were paraded on silver plates
for everyone to see, but none
recognised them except one –
Megacles who sat uppermost
on a table close to his host.

When he saw the infant items
he at once acknowledged them
though rocked with incredulity:
Ye Holy Gods! What do I see!
What has become of my child?

Does she live or has some clod
stumbled on her first chattels?
For pity's sake, Dionysophanes,
tell me how you retrieved
my daughter's clothes. Stint
not my luck after finding your
own son. For years I clawed
a living overspending on plays,
on travel, at public games;
and thus in poverty my child
was born and this is why
I despaired and could not care
for her; why I abandoned her
with these effects hoping another
would somehow chance upon her.
Placed in the Nymphs' Cave
I entrusted her to their care.
And now I am rich and grow
richer each day and yet have no
heir, not even a daughter.
The gods gave me no quarter
for what I did; they mocked me
in dreams parading a sheep
as her guardian in my place.

But Dionysophanes silenced
Megacles and swept him into
an inner ante-chamber to
deliver up Chloe dressed
in robes like a young empress.

Here is that very daughter
you abandoned! To amuse the
gods a sheep was her nurse
just as a goat suckled Daphnis.
Take your child again and her
goods, but then give her over

to be Daphnis's wife. We
both abandoned our babies
but have found them again.
Praise the Nymphs and Pan
for watching over them!

Megacles agreed and sent
for his wife Rhode to join
him and take Chloe home.
But she quickly returned to the
fields, for Daphnis and Chloe
found city life very strange.
And besides, it was arranged
that plain pastoral nuptials
would be best. And so they all
went to Lamo's humble house
where Megacles met Dryas,
Rhode made much of Nape and
the wedding feast was planned.
Then, at the feet of the Nymphs
Megacles gave Chloe to Daphnis
and, with other precious gifts,
her crucial birth belongings
were consecrated in the grotto;
and Dryas's sum was raised to
ten thousand drachmas in
respect of Chloe's rearing.

Theirs was a halcyon day.
Dionysophanes commanded
beds of leafy boughs to be
laid near the Cave; then he
invited the villagers to make
merry with Dryas and Nape,
Lamo and Myrtle, Dorco
and his kin and friends, also
Philetas and his son, Tityrus.
And neither was Lampis,

soon forgiven, absent; and
as is the custom when peasants
feast freely there were songs
and ribald revelry. They sang
the reaper's song and performed
the Epilenion – a madcap mime
usually staged at harvest.
A pipe was played by Philitas,
a flute by Lampis and Dryas
and Lamo danced while Daphnis
and Chloe hugged and kissed;
even the goats grazing close
were pricked by such hilarity.
And later others from the city
watched in wonder as Daphnis
named each goat and gripped
their horns to make them stand
and feed from his open hand.

Then night fell and the stars,
moon and planets hurrahed.
The married pair were squired
to their room in rush light
by pipes and flutes, and Daphnis
lay with Chloe skin against skin.
Cuddling tightly and kissing,
entwining and twisting
they slept less than two owls,
for Daphnis remembered well
Lycenia's lesson of love,
so that Chloe knew above
all else for the first time that
the giddy fumbling they had
foolishly fudged in the fields
was but the romping of puppies.

And for the rest of their days
they clung to their rural ways,
serving the gods: Eros, Pan
and the Nymphs, pleased to dine
on nothing but apples and milk,
and always took pains to deck
the grotto, erect statues above
and build their altars to Love.

~ The End ~

Dafydd ap Gwilym's poems

(c1320 to c1370)
translated cywyddau

Dafydd ap Gwilym was a 14th century minstrel poet and a contemporary of Chaucer. Both wrote in a century which boomed with the poetry of Petrarch, Dante and Boccaccio.

I happen to live in the village of Penrhyncoch very close to his birthplace at Brogynin, then in the parish of Llanbadarn now a suburb of Aberystwyth.You can still visit its ruins. He is traditionally buried under a yew tree at Strata Florida's Cistercian Abbey some 12 miles from there. Dafydd ap Gwilym is considered to be the one of the finest of all European Medieval poets and there is no doubt that his blend of the bardic tradition with more radical influences elevated Welsh poetry into the mainstream of European literature.

Very little is known of his life apart from local references in his verse. He appears to have been a troubadour from a good family but rarely travelled outside of Wales. His verse, steeped in the oral tradition and of course in Welsh, would have been memorised and recited to the accompaniment of a lute. He brought to the poetic formalities of the time a racy, colloquial style and a new light-heartedness (see *Trouble at the Inn*). But it's mainly because he avoided the usual topics of courtly love and legend, and wrote about whatever came to mind that he is so remarkable as a medieval poet.

Many of his poems were addressed to the love of his life, Morfudd, who inconveniently for him just happened to be married to a local Aberystwyth merchant (*Repentance*). Their dalliance went on for most of his life although some poems are addressed to another love interest – Dyddgu – who appears to have lived in North Wales. He wrote about the young women of Llanbadarn parish (*The Girls of Llanbadarn*) who wouldn't sleep with him. There are several devotional poems in his cannon and poems about birds (*The Owl*) and there's even a poem addressed to his penis (*My Todger*) which, he tells us, got him into a lot of trouble.

– *Nigel Humphreys*

Trafferth mewn Tafarn

Trouble at the Inn

I reached my favourite town
with my excellent liegeman.
Used to spending well on food,
well-heeled since boyhood, I took
decent lodgings; they were fine
and popular. I drank some wine
and spotted a winsome wench
in the inn, a honeybunch,
whose fair maiden hair shone
the colour of the dawn sun.
I bought a roast (not to boast)
for us both with wine that cost
me dear. Young men love to treat,
so I called her to where I sat
and we ate a meal of great taste,
better than any wedding feast.
Then, emboldened, I whispered
in her ear some fetching words,
and after the ice was thawed
by my sweet talk (a close call!),
and love being in the air, I made
a date to meet this feisty maid,
this loose-haired damsel, when
everybody else had turned in.

All was quiet and peaceful
except for myself and the girl
as I slyly sought out her bed.
But catastrophe and dread!
I fell over and yelled out
cursing love for poor sport;
and through my folly I hit

my shin hard, (my poor limb!)
on the edge of an idiot stool.
It was the innkeeper's bungle.
Being too eager is bad
and through the repeated
treachery of crashing about
my head gave the table a clout
causing a bowl and a brass pan
to reverberate and clang.
The table fell – a stout built
trestle – and its contents spilt
as the pan in agony died
and was heard far and wide.
The bowl joined in too (clumsy!)
as the inn dogs howled when I
sprang up in haste from the floor
with great noise (Wales for ever!),
for it was easier to rise knurly
like a clown than with dignity.

By the outer walls there stunk
three English men in one bunk
squirming on their haversacks:
Hicken and Jenkin and Jack.
The drunken one among them
hissed slyly in high dudgeon:

– There's Taff, set on knavery
crashing about with devilry.
He'll rob us if we let him;
keep clear of the bumpkin!

Then the landlord woke them all
bawling out a tragic tale
and set on at least nine to search
for me as if I were some wretch,
while I in my ugly bruises

kept silent in the darkness.
I prayed in my own small way
hush-hush as one in disarray,
and by the power of my prayer
for Jesus' tender care
in a dazed muddle I got back
to my bed without further mishap.
I had escaped thanks to the saints,
but begging the Lord's forgiveness.

Y Dylluan

The Owl

Riled I am that this shrill owl
is not silent, dead or at least ill;
will not let me say my prayers,
stay mute as the stars appear.
I cannot (ah, what nuisance!)
manage neither sleep nor peace.

Its hoot will storm a bat's home
even in the hail and snow.
Though once a joy to my ears
as my memory will swear,
when I close my eyes at night,
my venerable lords, it
awakens me and I cannot sleep
for its constant hooting, screech
and infernal noise, the guffaws
and wild harangues from its maw.
Must I suffer until dawn
like this from its vile foghorn,
its shrieking blood-curdling wails,
the too-wit-too-woo of its hail?

By Anna's kin, its cry incites
every town dog in the night.
Hellish it is with its infernal
hoot, large head and awful call;
this broad-browed, rowan-dyed,
wide-eyed catcher of mice;
this base, lacklustre insomniac.
Its tawny-downed, mucid yak-yak
whoops throughout all the woods,
beyond the farms and far wolds.
To you its face may seem kind
but in truth it's a ghoulish fiend.

Birds treat it as fugitive –
how odd that it has survived?
This one prates more on the hillside
than the forest nightingale at night.
Nor by day will it, this I know,
withdraw its head from its hollow.
Howling at will, I know its kith,
it is the bird of Gwyn ap Neath.
This crazy bird will sing to rogues,
I curse its tongue and fugues!

To drive this owl far from me
I have composed this poetry
and as I face the winter freeze
I'll also set alight its tree.

Merched Llanbadarn

The Girls of Llanbadarn

I am buckled with rage, a plague
on all the girls in this place!
For I've never had (cruel gems!)
a single one of them,
not a virgin (the sweetest itch),
nor damsel, shrew nor bitch!
What restraint, base infamy
or flaw stops them pawing me?
What would it harm a fair maid
to warm me in a dark glade?
It would be no disgrace for her
to love me in her leafy lair.

Never was a time I did not love,
never was a passion so restive;
lustier than Garwy's progeny
I could love one or two a day.
Yet I'm no nearer any of these
than if they were my enemies.
At church on every Sunday
in old Llanbadarn, they say,
I deify their daughters
with my back to the altar.

Once, after I'd ogled the flock
for what seemed like an epoch
I heard a lovely lass whisper
to her friend, wise and fair:

– He has a lecherous look,
his roving eye masks hemlock,
that pale boy with his come on
and a sister's hair on his crown!

– Is that what's on his mind?
asked the girl at her side.
– For my part he'll go without;
damn him, the lunatic lout!

I was stunned by her reproof:
a pittance for my dazzling love!
Perhaps I ought to abstain
from these doting idle dreams;
I'd best become a hermit:
a calling fit for culprits
since by my keen endeavours
(as a lesson for failed lovers)
it has fallen to me, a poet,
to be a wry-necked celibate.

Y Gal

My Todger

Todger, you must be manned
with vigilance, kept in hand
now more than ever thanks
to your pole-rodding pranks.
Twatprick! Because of a suit
I must muzzle your snout
to stop me being arraigned
again. Oh, my minstrel pain!

You are a foul rolling pin,
scrotum horn, ever out and in.
God's gift to all Christian girls,
a nut-hard pole for groin holes,
meet for mouths like the neck
of a young goose when stretched,
or a swollen teat for milking.
Lower your lance from tilting!
Bent, abhorrent broom stale,
a Doric column for a girl's tail.
A rearing sea snake spitting out,
your head blunt as a pig's snout.
Longer than a rabbit's thigh,
a battering ram to storm a sigh.
A drill with quick hard thrusts,
your plum-hued tip breeds disgust.
A crowbar to prise its worst,
a bolt shot across a girl's arse.
There's a tube inside your tool
to whistle up your daily pull.
You have a cockscomb's eye
which would make a harlot cry.
Pestle head, inflated artillery,
the curse of every tight cunny.
A thatching rod for female laps,

a direct conduit to the clap.
A sperm spar used for speed,
erectile tissue for casting seed.
You fill my hose with wantonness
leather-necked, scrag-end goose!
A scabbard for my ribald ego,
a nail to hang my writs and woe.

Think of me now being sued.
Shame on you, breeder of broods!
You are so difficult to restrain
even through a jerk's sudden pain!
Too often have I been besmeared
When your purple helmet's reared.

Edifeirwch

Repentance

As Morfudd's poet I despair
for it's hot work writing of her.
By He who commands the day
my head aches for the fair maid.
On my brow sit frets of distress;
I would die for my gilded mistress!
When, with the racking of bones
death comes in quicksilver groans
my human tongue will fail
and life's loss will be monumental.
Lest there be wailing and fury
let the Trinity and Virgin Mary
forgive my countless flaws.
Amen, I shall sing no more.

~ The End ~